T0358332

Cambridge Elements ≡

Elements in Business Strategy
edited by
J.-C. Spender
Kozminski University

DIGITAL ASSETS

A Portfolio Perspective

Henrique Schneider
Futurewave SICAV

Shaftesbury Road, Cambridge CB2 8EA, United Kingdom

One Liberty Plaza, 20th Floor, New York, NY 10006, USA

477 Williamstown Road, Port Melbourne, VIC 3207, Australia

314–321, 3rd Floor, Plot 3, Splendor Forum, Jasola District Centre,
New Delhi – 110025, India

103 Penang Road, #05–06/07, Visioncrest Commercial, Singapore 238467

Cambridge University Press is part of Cambridge University Press & Assessment,
a department of the University of Cambridge.

We share the University's mission to contribute to society through the pursuit of
education, learning and research at the highest international levels of excellence.

www.cambridge.org
Information on this title: www.cambridge.org/9781009500630

DOI: 10.1017/9781009437622

First published 2024

A catalogue record for this publication is available from the British Library.

ISBN 978-1-009-50063-0 Hardback
ISBN 978-1-009-43760-8 Paperback
ISSN 2515-0693 (online)
ISSN 2515-0685 (print)

Digital Assets

A Portfolio Perspective

Elements in Business Strategy

DOI: 10.1017/9781009437622
First published online: December 2024

Henrique Schneider
Futurewave SICAV

Author for correspondence: Henrique Schneider, hschneider@sigf.li

Abstract: From the perspective of an investor, digital assets are an alternative class of assets. They have several features that differentiate them from traditional investments. This makes them well-suited for a diversified portfolio. The question is how to accommodate them in such a portfolio, how to manage their potential and risk, and how to evaluate them. This short Element explains how to include digital assets is a diversified portfolio. It focuses on their differentiating use cases, their idiosyncracies, and how they relate to other types of investment. This is a Element for practitioners and students in finance, asset management, or portfolio construction.

This Element also has a video abstract: www.cambridge.org/EBUS_Schneider

Keywords: digital assets, crypto assets, blockchain, distributed ledger, decentralized finance, bitcoin

ISBNs: 9781009500630 (HB), 9781009437608 (PB), 9781009437622 (OC)
ISSNs: 2515-0693 (online), 2515-0685 (print)

Contents

1 Purpose

This Element is about using digital assets – also called crypto assets – from the portfolio's or investor's perspective. This Element aims to:

- Explain the underlying principles of digital assets.
- Differentiate between the use cases of digital assets and their respective value propositions.
- Expose different metrics, valuation methods, and risk models applicable to digital assets.
- Develop a framework for digital asset inclusion (or exclusion) in an investment portfolio.

You should read this Cambridge Elements on digital assets if you are:

- An investment professional, consultant, executive, and related interested in a practical approach to digital assets or
- Interested in the use cases of digital assets and the economics of this investment space or
- Curious about specific uses of digital assets, such as transactions and payments, decentralized finance, tokenization, and Web 3.0 or
- Studying or researching digital assets from an investment, management, or economic point of view.

1.1 To Know Digital Assets Is to Use Them

How do you use digital assets in an investment portfolio? Responding to this question involves addressing digital assets' use cases, value drivers, and risk profiles. In other words, understanding digital assets means knowing how to use them as an investment in a balanced portfolio. This Element calls this approach to digital assets a "pragmatist stance." It is pragmatic because it looks for the use of digital assets rather than their underlying technology. Naturally, the technology impacts the use case. But as an investor or a portfolio manager, the focus is to know how the digital asset behaves economically – opposite to technically.

This view has some implications. These are, in a nutshell: First, the pragmatist stance acknowledges a technical layer to the understanding of what digital assets are, but it maintains that, at least from the investment point of view, this layer is less important than the use of the digital asset in a market context or process. Naturally, there is a connection between technology and use, but not a deterministic one. For example, Bitcoin and Ethereum differ technically in substantial ways, but both can serve as means of payment. Even Ethereum's other uses are a function of the business case, not its technology. The use case of a digital asset is not determined by its technology but by its economic value added. The technology enables – not determines – adding value and is one of many aspects of a business case.

Second, according to the pragmatist stance, a digital asset's value and risk profile does not necessarily follow from its technical underlying but is the outcome of market processes. Market processes are how subjective preferences and information are aggregated by freely taken decisions to exchange, transforming them into valuations and creating welfare. In digital assets, one asset's specific network is the pivot for that asset's value and risk. For example, Bitcoin's widespread net of users is, at the same time, a driver of its value and the cause of its volatility. Technology can, of course, influence these value and risk profiles. But it remains one aspect among many. Again, a digital asset's specific value and risks depend on its business case and reception in market processes.

Finally, the pragmatist stance views digital assets as an evolving space. We are currently at the beginning of this development. Their use cases are still emerging; even the base technology can undergo several changes. At this stage – well, at any – it isn't easy to choose winners. Even risk assessment is challenging because of the limited timeframe and data volume. With the expansion of the digital assets space, solidifying use cases, and even accumulating its pitfalls and crises, investors will learn more about digital assets, and the models will improve.

1.2 Digital Assets Are Only as Good as Their Use Case

In principle, any investment creates value by making something consumers want. Financial assets facilitate this creation by mobilizing financial resources and directing them to venues for potential value creation. Financial investments often solve specific problems in market processes, such as bridging scarcity in capital, providing liquidity, enabling risk-takers to act, mitigating risk, qualifying and differentiating steps in the chain of value addition, and many more.

Digital assets, viewed as a type of financial investment, are not different. They, too, are addressing a specific need or problem in the market processes. The justification of any – investment-grade – single digital asset is whether it has a feasible business model that adds value and makes customers better off. This value add, or value proposition, is what investors look for when considering a digital asset. Simply put, a digital asset is only as good as its use case.

This Element identifies four layers of use cases. Section 3 discusses them and offers alternative views. CAIA, the Chartered Alternative Investment Analyst Association, developed these four layers. The CAIA has a dedicated program exploring digital assets. For that program, digital assets are understood as layers, each building upon the other. Shares and options are a loose analogy to that approach. Options are a layer of financial instruments presupposing, for example, publicly traded equity or shares. The rationale for CAIA's layering is that "portfolio-grade" investments in digital assets build upon the specific digital asset's use case and feasibility. These, in turn, are interconnected to their ecosystem in several ways. The CAIA's layers are:

- Payments, where the value proposition of digital assets is lowering transaction costs and monetizing investments via their commoditization.
- Token Currencies are digital securities or tokens used as a medium of exchange to store value or access services such as utilities, security, decentralized finance, governance, and non-fungible tokens.
- Decentralized finance, such as decentralized exchanges, oracles, digital lending and borrowing, insurance, yield farming, and derivatives, the value proposition of the digital asset being the elimination of intermediary, offering, instead, a rule-based, transparent, secure, and relatively cheap validation of transactions.
- The next version of the internet, sometimes called iteration, Web 3.0, promises customization of the web to the needs and preferences of the individual user. Gaming, social media, and the metaverse are applications of Web 3.0. The value proposition of digital assets here is to increase user control via Web 3.0 digital assets, payments, identity tools, and financial services.

1.3 Mosaic and Portfolio Approaches

This pragmatist view especially applies to investing in digital assets. Assessing their risk and using valuation methods cannot rely on a metric only. The complexity and dynamic of this investment space are best addressed when different metrics and methods complement each other. This mosaic approach is necessary to understand the multifaceted way in which digital assets create value.

Similarly, because they are multifaceted, investments in digital assets are better thought of within the logic of a portfolio. A portfolio is the combined holdings of various assets owned by an agent. The allocation of investments to the asset class of digital assets has repercussions on the total profile of all asset classes.

1.4 The Way Forward

This Element provides an overview of digital assets in a four-stepped approach. Each step follows in a separate section:

- Section 2 explains the principles of digital assets. While it reflects some of the technology underpinning the space, the task of the section is to achieve a pragmatist-level understanding by focusing on the governance mechanisms of distributed ledgers and blockchains.
- Section 3 expands on the use cases of digital assets. The pragmatist-level understating championed here submits that a digital asset's likelihood of success depends on its value proposition, that is, the real-world problem it solves.
- Section 4 explores risks regarding digital assets and methods for their valuation. Risk and valuation depend on whether an asset generates revenue or cash flow, a quality that separates mere tokens from decentralized finance.
- Section 5 discusses how to include digital assets in an investment portfolio.
- The conclusion is a checklist with a framework for investing in digital assets.

This is a short Element explaining the current state of the digital asset space. Each section, however, can be read independently and comes with a short overview of its contents and some references for further reading. In its content and structure, this Element follows the approach to digital assets favored by CAIA, the Chartered Alternative Investment Analyst Association, in its curriculum. There are other ways of treating this subject, but CAIA's comprehensive view corresponds well with the pragmatic understanding championed here.

To focus the reading of this Element on this pragmatist view, each section has a main premise or message:

- Section 2 claims that using a digital asset presupposes knowing its governance mechanisms.
- Section 3 submits that a digital asset can only create value if it can address users' needs to solve a real-world problem.
- Section 4 argues that a mosaic approach is needed in evaluating and evaluating a digital asset's risk profile.
- Section 5 posits that investments in digital assets should be seen in a portfolio approach involving all asset classes.

2 Principles of Digital Assets

Abstract: One must understand their underlying governance mechanisms to use digital assets effectively. Digital or crypto assets, existing solely in electronic form, serve as the foundational elements for decentralization across various sectors, notably finance. At its core, decentralization involves a peer-to-peer network validating transactions via digital protocols. These transactions are recorded on a distributed ledger – a blockchain. The consensus among these peers ensures transparency and trustworthiness by adding immutable records to the ledger.

Nevertheless, there is a challenge, often called the blockchain trilemma: achieving decentralization, security, and scalability is difficult. Various digital assets approach this challenge in distinct ways, often by modifying the consensus mechanism or using layered solutions. Within this realm, "tokenization" denotes blockchain's ability to represent ownership, while "smart contracts" are autonomous programs executing on these ledgers.

This section claims that using a digital asset presupposes knowing its governance mechanisms. It reviews the principles associated with digital assets. They are the principles of the governance of decentralization. This section discusses:

- Decentralization
- Governance
- Distributed ledger and blockchain
- Consensus mechanism
- Proof of Work and Proof of Stake
- The blockchain trilemma
- Layers of blockchains
- Tokenization
- Smart Contracts

The best way to read this section is to imagine it as a layered structure. It first relates very general principles and, with each section, deepens the level of analysis a bit. So, for example, if questions about how decentralization works are left open after reading the first section, the following section addresses them. This process continues in the subsequent ones. However, as this Element, this section is mainly concerned with how a portfolio manager or investor can use digital assets. It will, therefore, not go into details of information technology but remain on the level of governance because governance has a direct link to the economic use case of these assets.

2.1 Decentralization

The core promise of digital assets is a decentralized network. This network can be used for transactions in many realms, for example, finance, insurance, other legal contracts, and even in the verification trail needed to approve pharmaceuticals or scientific papers. Decentralization and networks go hand in hand. Instead of entrusting a central entity with responsibility, several entities do the same work in parallel. This work is to maintain an interconnected web. The whole network, maintained by these so-called nodes, takes over responsibility.

Decentralization, as proposed by digital assets, has several advantages. It reduces the risk of unauthorized manipulation or tampering with the records, relies on a consensus mechanism to maintain the records, and submits each intended change to scrutinize this mechanism, consisting of several peer-to-peer nodes. This layout also increases the decentralized system's resilience. Since there is no single point of failure, even if one or some nodes are attacked or fail, the others are left unaffected and can continue to maintain the system without losing information.

A decentralized system, as submitted by digital assets, operates with the immutability of its record-keeping and transparency. Each node stores the whole record of all transactions that have taken place in the network. Participants can independently verify the integrity of the records without going through a central agent or clearing house. Finally, decentralization makes it harder for any single entity or group to control specific transactions or data, let alone all transactions or data.

The decentralized system of digital assets operates a distributed ledger or the blockchain. It is, fundamentally, a way to store immutable data in chronological order. The storing of the data occurs when the several nodes maintaining this decentralized ledger agree on changing it, that is, adding information to it. This system is called the consensus mechanism that governs the network.

Sometimes, the decentralization of the networks of digital assets is said to be trustless. This "trustlessness" refers to the property of a system where participants can engage in transactions and interactions without needing to trust a central authority or intermediary. In traditional systems like financial institutions or centralized databases, users rely on trusted intermediaries to facilitate transactions and maintain records' accuracy. This trust can sometimes be problematic due to the potential for fraud, censorship, single points of failure, or abuse of power by the intermediaries. Distributed ledger technology, especially in public and decentralized blockchains, eliminates the need for trust in a central authority, thus achieving trustlessness. However, trustlessness only means the absence of the need for trust in singular entities. Participants in a network of digital assets trust the network as a system.

Distributed ledger technology is not new. In the late 1980s, Bell Laboratories hired Scott Stornetta, an American physicist, who was actively working to solve the problem of preventing the manipulation of data and information in scientific research. In the 1990s, Stornetta hired computer scientist and cryptographer Stuart Haber. Stornetta and Haber worked together on building a solution to this problem, which sought to create a timestamp verification system for documents. This timestamp would work by using a distributed ledger and cryptographic protocols. The idea behind the solution is that if anything within the document is changed, there would be an immutable trail that scientists could trace back to the original document.

In 2008, the first blockchain application, a specific version of the distributed ledger, was used to create Bitcoin based on Satoshi Nakamoto's whitepaper from 2008. The ignition for Bitcoin's idea was the Financial Crisis of 2007–2009. From the viewpoint of many agents, the crisis is one of trust in centralized systems – banks, insurers, and central banks. Bitcoin's core promise was establishing an alternative currency with decentralized, networked maintenance. Without needing to trust any singular intermediary, Bitcoin's value proposition is that participants can trust the network with its consensus mechanism and algorithm. Since 2009, digital assets have been using distributed ledger technology to deliver on their promise of decentralization. Specific use cases follow in the next section.

2.2 Governance

The principles associated with digital assets are best understood as the governance of decentralization, which enables digital assets to exist in digital or electronic form in a distributed ledger using cryptographic techniques to ensure security, authenticity, and ownership. The governance of digital assets generally shows the following characteristics – each being adaptable to a specific application or use case:

- Decentralization: Digital assets are typically based on a distributed ledger or blockchain technology. Unlike traditional centralized systems where a single authority controls the data, blockchain networks are maintained by several nodes, ensuring no single entity has complete control over the asset's information. This decentralization increases security, reduces the risk of single points of failure, and fosters trust in the system.
- Cryptography: Digital assets use cryptographic algorithms to secure transactions. In doing so, they also ensure and validate the control of ownership and governance implementation. Public-key cryptography is crucial in securing digital asset transactions, allowing users to generate a pair of cryptographic keys (public and private). The public key serves to receive assets, while the private key serves to access and transfer those assets securely.
- Transparency and Immutability: Distributed ledger networks are designed to be transparent and immutable. Every transaction involving a digital asset is recorded on the distributed ledger, and this information is publicly available for anyone to inspect. This transparency ensures accountability and trust among users and provides an auditable history of asset transactions.
- Ownership and Control: In digital assets, ownership is determined by possessing private keys. Users who own the private key associated with a digital asset's public address have complete control and ownership over the asset. This control eliminates the need for intermediaries like banks or financial institutions and empowers individuals to be their custodians.

In addition to these characteristics shared by almost every digital asset, some depend on the use case of the specific asset. The following elements do not need to be shared by every digital asset but are becoming quite common:

- Tokenization: Digital assets are often represented as tokens on blockchain networks. Tokenization allows real-world assets, such as real estate, art, or commodities, to be represented digitally as tokens. Agents can trade tokens on various blockchain platforms, making fractionalizing ownership easier and increasing liquidity in traditionally illiquid markets.

- Programmability (Smart Contracts): Often, smart contracts use distributed ledger technology. These contracts are self-executing contracts. Their terms are directly written into code. Digital assets on blockchain networks often support smart contracts, allowing developers to program complex rules and conditions that govern the behavior of the asset. This programmability enables the automation of various processes, such as payments, royalties, and asset distribution, without intermediaries.

- Interoperability: Digital assets can be compatible with different blockchain networks and platforms if standardization is part of the initial design. Standards like ERC-20 (Ethereum Request for Comments 20) enable interoperability, allowing tokens to be easily transferred between various applications and wallets, fostering a more interconnected and efficient ecosystem.

2.3 Distributed Ledger and Blockchain

The core of digital assets is the technological principle they operate, the distributed ledger, or, in most cases, the blockchain. These terms are often used synonymously, but some differences exist.

A **distributed ledger** is a database. Its main characteristic is that it exists simultaneously across multiple locations or nodes, where each node maintains a copy of the entire database. The distributed ledger is decentralized. No central agent or authority is controlling it. Instead, the responsibility for maintaining and validating the ledger is distributed among the network participants. They always strive to maintain an identical ledger copy via a consensus mechanism. The distributed ledger only works if the decentralized copies are identical. If the participants cannot agree, the ledger forks out, that is, it divides itself into agreements and nonagreements, each continuing a ledger of its own.

Features of the distributed ledger are:

- Decentralization: No single entity or central authority controls the entire ledger. Instead, multiple nodes contribute to the maintenance and validation of the database.

- Protocol: A protocol is a simple set of rules run by computers that allow data or transactions to take place.
- Consensus Mechanism: To ensure the accuracy and consistency of the ledger, distributed ledgers use various consensus mechanisms to agree on the state of the database and validate transactions – they will be discussed in more detail later in this section.
- Transparency: Participants in the network can access and verify the data on the distributed ledger. This transparency enhances trust among participants and allows for auditing and verification of transactions.
- Immutability: It is immutable once data are added to the distributed ledger. That is, it cannot be altered or deleted; it can only be amended. Changes to the ledger must be agreed upon by the network participants, providing a solid level of security and integrity.

Blockchains are specific implementations of distributed ledger technology. Using cryptographic hashes, the blockchain organizes data into blocks linked together in chronological order. Each block contains a list of entries (transactions) and the previous block's hash. This chaining of blocks creates an unbroken and tamper-resistant chain of data.

Specific features of the blockchain, that is, in addition to the general characteristics of the distributed ledger, are:

- Block Structure: Data are organized into blocks, and each block contains a cryptographic hash, which acts as a unique identifier, a reference to the previous block, creating a chronological chain of information, which is generated based on the data in the block.
- Cryptographic Security: Blockchain uses cryptographic techniques, such as the interplay of private and public keys, to secure transactions, ensuring that only the rightful owner of the private key can access and transfer digital assets.

The blockchain allows for further differentiation regarding the group of people who have access to a specific network:

- Public blockchains are open-source and allow anyone to access them. Transactions on a public blockchain are transparent to all participants, and consensus is usually achieved through computational methods or a voting mechanism.
- Private blockchains are exclusive networks that require permission to access and participate. Transactions on a private blockchain may not be visible to all participants, and the license can be revoked or given at any time by a centralized party or consortium. These permissioned blockchains are used in enterprise solutions where the operator requires more control.

- Hybrid or consortium blockchains borrow characteristics from both public and private ones but tend to be lumped in with private ones.

In summary, a distributed ledger is a general concept describing a database that exists across multiple locations and is maintained decentralized. Blockchain is a specific implementation of a distributed ledger that organizes data into blocks and uses cryptographic hashing for linking blocks together. As mentioned earlier, blockchain is just one implementation of distributed ledger technology. Still, it is the most widely used and the basis for many cryptocurrencies and other forms of digital assets. Its potential applications in various industries are promising, too.

2.4 Consensus Mechanism

The core of the governance of the distributed ledger is its consensus mechanism. It is a set of rules enabling participants in a specific blockchain network to agree. Agreeing means validating transactions and reaching a consistent view of the ledger's state. The consensus mechanism works without the need for a central authority.

A feature of decentralization is its governance by the consensus of its nodes. This governance must be organized, that is, providing for a process through which a network's nodes come to a consensus on the order and content of transactions, maintaining the integrity and security of the distributed ledger system.

Next to the general issues about governance and network maintenance, the consensus mechanism must also solve the so-called double-spending problem. How do you ensure that a digital asset unit is transacted only once?

In decentralized digital asset systems, there is no central authority or trusted intermediary to validate transactions. Instead, these systems rely on consensus mechanisms to achieve agreement among network participants about the validity of transactions.

The double-spending problem arises because digital data can be easily copied, and there is no physical constraint to prevent someone from spending the same digital asset multiple times. For example, if someone were to send the same cryptocurrency token to two different recipients in rapid succession, there would be no inherent mechanism to prevent this duplication – unless there is a governance of the network, the consensus mechanism. Decentralized digital asset systems use consensus protocols to address the double-spending problem. They reach an agreement on the valid state of the ledger. A transaction is only recognized as such if most nodes or validators agree.

Contemporarily, the most widely used consensus mechanisms are – their explanation will be expanded in the next section:

- Proof of Work, PoW, is the original and most well-known consensus mechanism used by Bitcoin and many other cryptocurrencies. Miners compete to solve complex mathematical puzzles embedded in the algorithm – solving these puzzles also maintains the network and is thus called "work." The first miner to find the correct solution adds a new block to this specific blockchain, receiving the block's rewards. PoW is known for its security but requires significant computational power and energy consumption. Bitcoin is an example of a network using PoW.
- Proof of Stake, PoS, relies on validators who are chosen to create blocks and validate transactions based on the number of assets of the ledge they "stake" or lock up as collateral. This system incentivizes validators to act honestly; they risk losing their staked assets if they behave maliciously. PoS is considered more energy efficient than PoW but may raise concerns about centralization based on wealth concentration. Ethereum 2.0 uses proof of stake. Others using PoS include Tezos, Cardano, Solana, and Algorand.

Other consensus mechanisms are:

- Delegated Proof of Stake, DPoS, is a variation of PoS where token holders can vote to elect a limited number of delegates or validators who have the right to create blocks and validate transactions on behalf of the network. DPoS aims to increase scalability by reducing the number of validators while maintaining decentralization through community voting. Steem, Lisk, and Bitshares use DPoS.
- Nominated Proof of Stake, NPoS, combines PoS and DPoS. Network participants nominate validators responsible for validating transactions and creating new blocks. This method reduces energy consumption and is supposed to enhance security and decentralization. An example for a network with NPoS is Polkadot.
- Proof of Authority, PoA, is a consensus mechanism where block validators are identified and authorized by a central authority or a set of approved entities. Validators are known entities, and the network's security relies on their reputation and accountability. PoA is used in private and consortium blockchains prioritizing efficiency and scalability over decentralization. For this reason, PoA cannot be considered part of a decentralized ledger. JP Morgan uses PoA for its JPMCoin.
- Proof of Space, PoSpace, is a consensus mechanism that leverages unused storage space on participants' devices to create proofs and participate in block creation. It relies on providing proofs of precomputed data, making it a more efficient alternative to PoW regarding energy consumption. BurstCoin uses the PoSpace.
- Proof of Burn, PoB, requires participants to burn or destroy a certain amount of digital assets of the network, sending them to a lock-up address. By doing

so, participants demonstrate their commitment to the network and earn the right to create blocks and participate in consensus. Namecoin users must destroy some bitcoins to participate in Namecoin's proof of burn system.

• Proof of Elapsed Time, PoET, is a consensus mechanism that aims to achieve randomness and leader selection fairly. Participants wait for a randomly generated timer to expire, and the one with the shortest time is selected as the leader to create the next block. Hyperledger Sawtooth, a permissioned network, uses it.

• Practical Byzantine Fault Tolerance, PBFT, is a consensus mechanism used in permissioned blockchains where network participants are known and trusted. It focuses on reaching a consensus in the presence of faulty or malicious nodes, ensuring the network can tolerate Byzantine failures. Blockchains like Zilliqa, Hyperledger fabric, and Tendermint use PBFT.

• Honey Badger Byzantine Fault Tolerance, HBBFT, is a consensus mechanism that achieves Byzantine fault tolerance without relying on a leader or coordinator. It uses cryptographic techniques and a network of nodes to reach consensus in an asynchronous network.

2.5 Proof of Work – Proof of Stake

Proof of Work and Proof of Stake are currently the most widely used consensus mechanisms. They differ in many ways from each other.

Proof of Work, PoW, is the original consensus mechanism introduced by Bitcoin and is widely used in several digital assets. In PoW, agents called miners compete to solve complex mathematical puzzles. Solving them means adding new blocks to the blockchain. The first miner who finds the correct solution adds the block to the blockchain, receiving newly minted cryptocurrency and transaction fees as a reward.

Thus, mining is the name of solving the puzzle embedded in the algorithm while maintaining the network. Miners use computational power to perform millions of calculations per second to find a hash value that meets specific criteria. Only once a node finds a hash (i.e., a viable input) that satisfies the output requirements, defined by the number of leading zeros in the output hash, can the block be finalized by that node and added to the chain, thus earning the node a block reward. The mining process is resource-intensive, requiring substantial computational power and energy consumption.

The mining puzzle's difficulty is regularly adjusted based on the network's total computational power. This setup ensures that new blocks are added roughly every ten minutes (in the case of Bitcoin) regardless of the number of miners or their combined computational power. Many PoW algorithms contain so-called halving, which increases the difficulties of mining. In the case of Bitcoin, the protocol is designed to undergo a halving approximately every four years, or more specifically, every 210,000 blocks. When a halving occurs, Bitcoin miners' reward for validating transactions, that is, adding them to the blockchain, is cut in half. This reduction in the block reward leads to a decreased rate of new Bitcoin entering circulation.

There are instances of divergence between the transaction history favored by nodes. This problem occurs when some of the network's participants cannot agree on the rules governing the blockchain's protocol or when there are conflicting views on how the blockchain should progress. In these cases, the blockchain forks.

A hard fork is a permanent and irreversible split in the blockchain's history, creating two independent and incompatible blockchains. It happens when a substantial change is made to the underlying protocol rules, and the nodes running the previous software version cannot validate transactions on the new version, and vice versa. Hard forks often require all participants to upgrade to the latest version of the blockchain's specific software to stay on the same chain.

Soft forks are less disruptive and contentious than hard ones, as they do not result in a permanent split in the blockchain's history. However, they may still require most network participants to adopt the upgraded software to ensure smooth consensus.

Forks, whether hard or soft, are a natural part of blockchain's evolution, allowing for improvements, scalability enhancements, and the implementation of new features. The specific outcome and impact of a fork depend on the community's response, the support from miners and nodes, and the reasons behind the fork.

Generally, PoW is considered secure because it requires significant computational work to reverse or alter transactions in previous blocks. An attacker would need to control more than half of the network's computational power (a 51 percent attack) to undermine the system, making it highly impractical in large, established networks. Proof of Work's main drawbacks are its high energy consumption and the competition for mining rewards, which can lead to centralization in mining pools.

Proof of Stake, PoS, is the main alternative to PoW, aiming to improve energy efficiency and counter-centralization issues. In PoS, validators are the entities maintaining the blockchain. They are chosen based on the number of the specific chain's coins or tokens they "stake" or "lock up" as collateral.

The probability of a validator being chosen to create a block is directly proportional to the number of coins they have staked. In other words, the more coins a validator locks up as collateral, the higher their chances of being selected.

In PoS, validators are incentivized to act honestly because they have a financial stake in the network. If a validator behaves maliciously or tries to attack the network, they risk losing their staked coins.

Proof of Stake is considered more energy efficient than PoW because it eliminates the need for resource-intensive mining. Validators must only maintain a running node to participate in block creation and transaction validation.

There are different variations of PoS, such as Delegated Proof of Stake DPoS, where token holders delegate their voting power to their representatives to create blocks on their behalf.

Critics argue that PoS might lead to centralization based on wealth concentration, as those with the most coins are more likely to be selected as validators. However, some PoS protocols implement mechanisms to mitigate this risk, such as limiting a single validator's maximum stake.

2.6 The Blockchain Trilemma

Distributed ledgers or blockchains face scalability–security–decentralization trilemma. It refers to the inherent trade-offs among these three critical attributes in distributed ledger and blockchain systems:

- Scalability refers to a blockchain's ability to handle many transactions quickly and efficiently. As more users join a blockchain network and the volume of transactions increases, the system must be able to process these transactions without significant delays or bottlenecks. Scalability is essential for mass adoption and blockchain applications requiring high throughput.
- Security is paramount in blockchain systems. It ensures that the data stored on the blockchain are tamper-resistant and that transactions are valid and trustworthy. The more security, the more capacity and energy miners and validators need to input in the maintenance of the network.
- Decentralization distributes control and the power to make decisions across a network's nodes or participants. The more decentralized a network operates, the more nodes it needs and, therefore, the more miners or validators.

The blockchain trilemma posits that a distributed ledger cannot maximize all three attributes simultaneously or with the same prioritization. Improving one aspect means lessening at least one of the others. For example:

- Suppose a blockchain prioritizes scalability by processing many transactions quickly. In that case, it may require larger blocks or faster block times, which can compromise decentralization as only powerful nodes can handle the increased resource requirements.

- If a blockchain prioritizes decentralization by encouraging participation from many nodes, it may lead to slower consensus and reduced scalability, as reaching agreement among numerous nodes takes more time.
- If a blockchain prioritizes security by employing a highly robust consensus mechanism, it may lead to slower transaction processing and limited scalability as the complexity of achieving consensus increases.

Various blockchain projects attempt to strike a balance between these three attributes, but it remains challenging. Different blockchain platforms have adopted different strategies, with some prioritizing certain characteristics over others based on the specific use cases they aim to address. The trilemma serves as a reminder that blockchain design involves making thoughtful trade-offs to achieve the desired characteristics for a particular application. Here are three examples of such decisions:

- With its upgrade 2.0, Ethereum transitioned from PoW to PoS. As the popularity of Ethereum grew, the network became congested, leading to high fees and slower transaction times. Changing its consensus mechanism to PoS is expected to provide better scalability. Scalability means more transactions can be processed in parallel, improving network performance. Also, this change is supposed to make the network more energy efficient.
- Bitcoin uses its PoW consensus mechanism because of its commitment to decentralization and security. Understanding that this commitment might be detrimental to scalability, the network prioritizes two aspects of the trilemma at the expense of the third. Bitcoin, intended to be (or become) a hard currency, values security and decentralization higher than its scalability. However, the Bitcoin community has explored so-called second-layer solutions like the Lightning Network to address scalability without compromising the base layer's security and decentralization. This is expanded in the next section.
- Several digital assets solve the trilemma by building upon an existing blockchain, which is then called layer one, and developing its network on top of it, which is then called layer two. The second layer prioritizes those aspects of the trilemma that are not addressed by the first, thus complementing it.

Ethereum and Bitcoin will be discussed in the next section. Layering is the object of the following section.

2.7 Layers of Blockchains

A blockchain ecosystem can consist of several layers. Each layer describes different levels or components of a blockchain ecosystem, that is, a system combining the strengths of two or more distributed ledgers.

A **layer zero** protocol forms the foundation for constructing layer one blockchains. Layer zero enables developers to launch customized layer one blockchains for specific applications or use cases. A layer zero mainchain supports the data transfer between layer one blockchains, while layer zero sidechains are application-specific layer one chains connected to the mainchain. Cosmos, Polkadot, and Avalanche are examples of layer zero ecosystems. Layer zero is among the most novel developments in the digital asset space. Observers think that it has one of the most significant innovative potentials.

A **layer one** blockchain refers to the primary or foundational blockchain protocol. It is the base layer of the blockchain system and includes the leading blockchain network and its native cryptocurrency. Layer one blockchains are responsible for managing the fundamental aspects of the network, such as consensus mechanisms, transaction validation, and security. Some well-known examples of layer one blockchains include Bitcoin BTC, Ethereum ETH, and Litecoin LTC.

Critical characteristics of layer one blockchains are:

- Security: Layer one blockchain relies on its security mechanisms, such as PoW in Bitcoin or Ethereum's transition to Proof-of-Stake (PoS), to achieve consensus and validate transactions.
- Decentralization: Layer one blockchains typically aim for high levels of decentralization, meaning that no single entity has complete control over the network.
- Native Currency: Layer one blockchains have their native cryptocurrencies used for various purposes, including transaction fees and securing the network through staking or mining.
- Limited Scalability: Many layer one blockchains face scalability challenges, meaning they have a limited capacity to process many transactions quickly and efficiently.

A **layer two** blockchain is a secondary blockchain protocol that operates on top of the layer one blockchain. It is designed to complement and enhance the functionalities of the layer one blockchain, addressing some of the scalability and performance issues associated with the primary blockchain. Layer two solutions are often implemented to increase transaction throughput and improve user experience without changing the underlying layer one protocol. Some examples of layer two solutions include the Lightning Network for Bitcoin and various scaling solutions (e.g., Plasma, Rollups) for Ethereum.

Critical characteristics of layer two blockchains are:

- Scalability: Layer two solutions are specifically designed to improve the scalability of the underlying layer one blockchain. By moving certain transactions off-chain or optimizing the way transactions are processed, they can achieve higher transaction throughput.

- Interoperability: Layer two solutions usually maintain a strong connection with the layer one blockchain, allowing users to move assets between the two layers seamlessly.
- Reduced Costs and Latency: By offloading some of the processing to the secondary layer, layer two blockchains can reduce transaction costs and decrease confirmation times.

2.8 Tokenization

Tokenization allows for establishing a link between a real-world asset and a digital asset. It is a process in which digital tokens are issued by and in a blockchain. These tokens represent ownership, rights, or access to specific assets, and they are typically created, managed, and transferred using smart contracts on a blockchain platform.

Tokens are usually distinguished by their fungibility. In digital assets, a fungible token is one where each unit is the same as every other. This means they are interchangeable. For example, one Bitcoin is the same as any other Bitcoin, just as one US-Dollar is the same as any other US-Dollar.

A non-fungible token NFT corresponds to a unique asset or piece of content on a blockchain. Each NFT is one-of-a-kind or part of a limited edition, and it has a unique set of data. This data could represent ownership details, metadata, and other information differentiating one NFT. Non-fungible tokens use blockchain technology to create, verify, or assert ownership and prove authenticity. The ownership of an NFT is recorded on the blockchain, making it easily traceable and verifiable. Non-fungible tokens are indivisible, meaning they cannot be divided into smaller units like cryptocurrencies. They exist as whole tokens and represent the entirety of the asset they are associated with.

Indivisibility, however, is a property of the token. The asset can be divided into a series of tokens. Tokenization can also allow for fractional ownership of assets, that is, to be divided into smaller units. For example, a real estate property worth millions of dollars can be tokenized into smaller fractions, making it accessible to a broader range of investors.

2.9 Smart Contracts

A smart contract is a code or program that automatically enforces and executes the terms of an agreement or contract when certain predefined conditions are met. This automatic enforcement is also called self-executing. These contracts are coded onto a blockchain platform, such as Ethereum, and are executed without the need for intermediaries or third-party involvement. Smart contracts operate based on predefined rules; once deployed on the blockchain, they cannot be altered or tampered with. These contracts can be used for various applications, including financial transactions, supply chain management, real estate transactions, insurance claims, and voting systems.

As with most blockchain applications, the terms and conditions of a smart contract are written in code and are visible to all participants on the blockchain. This transparency clarifies the contract's execution and helps avoid disputes regarding its interpretation. When specific conditions in the code are satisfied, the sum of transparency and the autonomous, self-executing contract eliminates the need for intermediaries, reduces the potential for human error, and ensures the contract is executed as intended. Smart contracts eliminate the need for intermediaries. They reduce costs and processing times associated with traditional contract enforcement. The automation of contract execution streamlines the process and reduces administrative overhead.

3 Use Cases in Digital Assets

Abstract: A digital asset can only create value if it can address users' needs to solve a real-world problem. Digital assets explain how they work and their value proposition in a whitepaper. There are already several use cases for digital assets. Clustering them is always an exercise in depicting the status quo. Since the use cases can develop quickly, any clustering is provisional. Following CAIA (*Digital Assets Microcredential*, 2023), use cases can be understood as payments, decentralized finance, token currencies, and Web 3.0. The CAIA's terminology sees these use cases as superimposed layers. However, grouping use cases differently is helpful, too, in understanding the breadth of use cases. Bitcoin is the first and paramount use case of a currency. Ethereum is a basic technology for smart contracts, including currencies. Decentralized finance is a term referring to financial investments without intermediaries. Finally, Web 3.0 is the new internet iteration with more user sovereignty.

This section submits that a digital asset can only create value if it can address users' needs to solve a real-world problem. It discusses some use cases in digital assets. While overviews are helpful for systematically understanding the value proposition of a distributed ledger, the analysis of specific cases reveals how the value proposition works, how it addresses some needs in the real world, and how it adds value in doing so. This section discusses the following topics:

- Whitepaper
- Clustering use cases

- Layering use cases
- Bitcoin
- Ethereum
- Payments and stablecoins
- Decentralized Finance
- Tokens
- Web 3.0

The section on whitepapers is a general overview of the information needed to assess a use case and where to find it. The section on clustering addresses the different grouping of use cases. This is continued in the section on CAIA's layering use cases. Following CAIA (2023), the sections on Bitcoin, Ethereum, and payments and stablecoins discuss digital assets as payment systems, paying attention to Ethereum's other use cases. The last remaining sections discuss the other layers of use cases of digital assets.

3.1 Whitepaper

In digital assets, a whitepaper is a comprehensive and detailed document that explains a particular project or digital asset. The goal of the whitepaper is to answer two questions about a specific project: **How does it work? What is the project's value proposition or use case?**

The whitepaper serves as an informational and technical blueprint for the project, outlining its purpose, underlying technology, features, use cases, and potential benefits. The creators or development teams of the digital asset typically release whitepapers. They are intended to inform potential investors, users, and the broader community about the project's goals and how it aims to achieve them. The usual components of a whitepaper are:

- Introduction: An overview of the project's goals, objectives, and the problem it aims to solve.
- Technology: A detailed explanation of the underlying technology, including the blockchain protocol, consensus mechanism, and other technical aspects relevant to the project.
- Use Cases / Value Proposition: A description of the digital asset's real-world applications and potential use cases.
- Tokenomics: Information about the cryptocurrency or token associated with the project, including its distribution, total supply, and token utility or governance features.
- Roadmap: A timeline that outlines the project's development milestones and future.

- Team: Information about the core team members, their backgrounds, and relevant expertise.
- Legal and Regulatory Considerations: A section that addresses any legal and compliance aspects related to the project and its token.

Investors refer to whitepapers to assess the viability and potential of a digital asset before deciding to invest, use, or support the project. However, it's important to note that not all whitepapers are created equal, and some may lack sufficient substance or even be misleading.

The first whitepaper for any digital asset was published on October 31st, 2008, by an individual or a group named **Satoshi Nakamoto** in a cryptography mailing list on a platform called Metzdowd. Its abstract reads:

> A purely peer-to-peer version of electronic cash would allow online payments to be sent directly from one party to another without going through a financial institution. Digital signatures provide part of the solution, but the main benefits are lost if a trusted third party is still required to prevent double-spending. We propose a solution to the double-spending problem using a peer-to-peer network. The network timestamps transactions by hashing them into an ongoing chain of hash-based proof-of-work, forming a record that cannot be changed without redoing the proof-of-work. The longest chain not only serves as proof of the sequence of events witnessed, but proof that it came from the largest pool of CPU power. As long as a majority of CPU power is controlled by nodes that are not cooperating to attack the network, they'll generate the longest chain and outpace attackers. The network itself requires minimal structure. Messages are broadcast on a best effort basis, and nodes can leave and rejoin the network at will, accepting the longest proof-of-work chain as proof of what happened while they were gone.

3.2 Clustering Use Cases

The best-known use cases in digital assets are Bitcoin as a currency and Ethereum as a basis technology for smart contracts. Before discussing them in detail, it is helpful to provide an overview of the needs distributed ledger technologies satisfy. After all, the value-added feature of business models is adding real-world customer situations.

At the end of 2022, there were 22,126 digital assets in existence (CAIA 2023). The sheer number of available assets can seem chaotic and complicated to filter down, and many of them will likely be consolidated or no longer exist over time. However, some common, albeit emerging, categorizations can be used better to understand the use cases of different protocols.

Any systematization of the different value propositions using distributed ledgers reflects the status quo. The distributed ledger space is fast-paced and develops quickly. Therefore, clustering exercises are always incomplete and provisional. Nonetheless, clustering helps understand the variety and breadth of applications. Taken with a grain of salt, they help identify current and future investment potential. This section discusses two different attempts at clustering.

The first clustering is a **catalog approach** proposed by Zīle and Strazdiņa (2018, 15). They group uses cases into four categories, each with several subcategories:

Data Management

- Network Infrastructure
- Content and resource distribution
- Cloud storage
- Data Monitoring
- Identity data management
- Contract management
- Interorganizational data management
- Tamper-proof event log and audit trail
- System metadata storage
- Data replication and protection from deleting
- Digital content publishing and selling
- Internet of Things sensor data purchasing

Data Verification

- Photo and video proofing
- Document notarization
- Work history verification
- Academic certification
- Identity verification and key management
- Product quality verification
- Proof of origin

Financial

- Cryptocurrency
- Stock share and bond issuing
- Trade Finance
- Currency exchange and remittance
- Peer–to–Peer payments

- Crowdfunding
- Insurance
- Supply chain management
- Value transfer and lending
- Investments in art
- Central bank money issuing

Community

- Prediction recording
- Social voting system
- Ridesharing
- Domain name registration
- Healthcare record storing
- Software license validation
- Content or product timestamping
- Lottery
- Property rights registration
- Social rating creation and monitoring
- Voting
- Marriage registration
- Court proceedings
- Donations
- Electronic locks
- Gaming
- Reviews and endorsement
- Product tracing
- Outsourcing of computational power

The second clustering uses a **matrix**-style approach, combining two dimensions or axes (Labazova et al. 2021, 9). There are three matrices. First, the dimension "governance of the blockchain" – decentralized, hybrid, centralized – is combined with its "application area" – financial transactions, enforcements, asset management, storage, communication, and ranking. In the second, one axis is the "application areas," and the other is the "properties of the blockchain" – token, customizability, data type, and history detention. In the third matrix, the "governance of the block-chain" is brought together with the "deployment of the blockchain" – access, validation, consensus mechanism, and anonymity level.

Each matrix serves a different purpose. The second and third help set up a business model based on a distributed ledger. The first matrix clusters different use cases as follows – along the axis application and governance:

- Financial Transaction

  - Decentralized: Cryptocurrency, Wealth Storage, Micro-Payments
  - Hybrid: Cross-Border and Interorganizational Payments
  - Centralized: Central-issued financial instruments

- Enforcements

  - Decentralized: Enforcement between individuals
  - Hybrid: Interorganizational Enforcement
  - Centralized: Central-Issued Enforcement

- Asset Management

  - Decentralized: Authentication, Ownership, Audit trails, access management
  - Hybrid: Interorganizational asset management
  - Centralized: enterprise asset management

- Storage

  - Decentralized: decentralized storage
  - Hybrid and centralized: not explored for blockchain systems

- Communication

  - Decentralized: Messengers, Internet of Things Communication
  - Hybrid and centralized: not explored for blockchain systems

- Ranking

  - Decentralized: Reputation, Rating
  - Hybrid and centralized: not explored for blockchain systems

3.3 Layering Use Cases

The **Chartered Alternative Investment Analyst Association** CAIA, the global professional body for the alternative investment industry, takes a different view. Instead of clustering digital assets in different groups, they are pictured as **layers**. The idea is that there are several ways of using digital assets, some of them presupposing others. Much like a telecommunications network in which several layers of technology and service levels are integrated or like some financial assets based upon other financial assets, digital assets are best understood as business models that are often integrated or which build on each other.

For example, payments are the simplest forms of digital assets. Decentralized finance uses the payments technology and networks but pushes them further,

.

expanding products and services. Web 3.0 relies on decentralized finance, which relies on payments, to expand the use case and the business model even further. The CAIA identifies four layers:

- **Payments** include stablecoins, central bank digital currencies, and credit card payments.
- **Decentralized finance**, DeFi, including decentralized exchanges, oracles, digital lending and borrowing, insurance, yield farming, and derivatives.
- **Token Currencies** are a medium of exchange, a store of value, and a way to access services.
- **Web 3.0** is a development of the internet in which users can monetize their content.

Chartered Alternative Investment Analyst Association's by-inclusion approach reflects the provisional character of any grouping. It looks at use cases from the point of view of investors and portfolio allocators. This section will broadly follow CAIA's view, addressing specific use cases in more detail.

Including a specific use case in a layer does not mean it has no similarity or connection. Instead, layers identify the primary function of a blockchain in its value-adding business model. This main function might build upon other functions and be integrated with them. In DeFi, for example, there are payments. But the blockchain's main function is to facilitate financial transactions. The DeFi layer builds on the payment layer.

The following sections will each introduce the use case, explaining them by responding to two questions: **How does it work? What is its value proposition?**

3.4 Bitcoin

Bitcoin is a global network that allows two parties to transfer value in the network's currency – bitcoin – directly with one another without any intermediary. Transactions are executed by adding information about the transactions to Bitcoin's blockchain, a decentralized, transparent, and immutable ledger of all Bitcoin transactions.

At the heart of Bitcoin is the loss of trust in centralized financial systems during and after the Financial Crisis of 2007–2008. With the bankruptcy or rescue of banks and insurers and the expansion of the monetary base for fiat currencies, Bitcoin's two core promises emerge: First, to establish a hard currency – more about this in the next section; and second, to remove third parties and intermediaries from financial transactions.

This second promise is "trustlessness." However, this label is only correct if applied to the user's trust in the intermediary. As a decentralized network, the

Bitcoin blockchain does not have third parties and, therefore, does not need any trust in a single intermediary entity. Participants transact directly with each other using the whole network, which is composed of several nodes. Participants send bitcoins or fractions thereof to each other using a combination of private and public keys once the transaction is cryptographically prepared and broadcast to the network, where its nodes validate it.

Despite "trustlessness" in individual intermediaries, the blockchain's participants need to trust the network, that is, its ability to enable transactions, keep track of them, avoid double counting and double-spending, stay secure, and maintain its resilience. This trust is generated by the network's nodes managing the blockchain – without changing the original algorithm – via a consensus and incentive mechanism called mining.

How does the Bitcoin blockchain work? Every transaction on the Bitcoin blockchain needs to be recorded by every node of the network – each operating independently from the other – to maintain a common ledger of balances and transactions. Bitcoin mining is batching new transactions, confirming them, and adding a new block with these transactions to the blockchain.

While batching these new transactions, miners must solve mathematical puzzles embedded into the Bitcoin algorithm. Solving these puzzles, processing transactions, validating them, and adding them to the chain, occur simultaneously. In performing these tasks, miners solve the puzzles. The miner who finds a solution announces it to the rest of the network, and the rest of the nodes check for its validity. While it is challenging to solve the puzzle, it is relatively easy to validate the result. When most of the nodes agree on the validity of a solution, the mined block is added to the chain, releasing the new bitcoin to the miner who came up with the answer.

This process has two incentives for complying with the consensus mechanism. First, most other nodes would only validate if a miner or node submits the right blocks. The computing power and resources invested in wrongly submitting would be lost. Second, should an agent be interested in corrupting the blockchain by altering it illegitimately, they would need to control 51 percent of the nodes. Again, measured in computing power and resources, orchestrating this 51 percent attack is too expensive compared to its reward.

Bitcoin gains robustness over time. The amount of mining power on the network is the hash rate. The higher the hash rate, the higher the puzzle's difficulty in maintaining the average Bitcoin block time of ten minutes. The difficulty is adjusted every 2016 block, at the current rate, approximately every two weeks. As new blocks are added to the blockchain, the transactions they contain become increasingly difficult to reverse, making it more reliable and secure over time.

Bitcoin's currency, the bitcoin, is supposed to be a hard currency and to increase its value over time. Hard is meant to be an alternative to fiat money, that is, a currency controlled by a central agent such as the central bank or a government. Fiat money allows this central agent unconstrained power over the currency, for example, to dilute, cancel, or change it. The hard currency is tied to a guarantee of value that cannot be influenced.

For this reason, the supply of bitcoins is capped at 21 million units, which are gradually released into circulation over time. (Over 19 million units are already in circulation, with less than 2 million to mine.) The cap is the un-influenceable guarantee of the value and soundness of the bitcoin. The number of new Bitcoins released per block decreases over time according to a predetermined "halving" schedule in which the number of Bitcoins that are created every block is cut in half after every 210,000 blocks. This halving takes approximately four years, as a new Bitcoin block is created approximately every ten minutes. The last Bitcoin is expected to be mined around the year 2140.

The fixed supply of Bitcoin and the decreasing rate at which new Bitcoin is released are intended to create a predictable and stable supply. When this cap is reached, market forces alone will determine the value of the bitcoin. This deflationary nature of Bitcoin is supposed to drive the value of the single unit, turning it into more than a means of payment but also a store of value. Note that the cap also means that eventually, there will be no more newly minted Bitcoin, and at that point, miners will be entirely compensated in the form of transaction fees.

What is the value proposition of Bitcoin? Bitcoin is meant to be a hard currency means of exchange. However, bitcoin is best understood as digital cash. Owning a Bitcoin means storing a token in a wallet – not just a claim on some entry in a balance sheet. While the token's validity is a matter of its place in the blockchain, the token, as such, is in the user's possession, changing this possession as a transaction is concluded – much like a banknote changes hands when paying in cash.

When compared with electronic transfers of funds facilitated by banks – also called a wire transfer, bank transfer, or credit transfer – Bitcoin has several advantages. While the sender and receiver must have a bank account for a wire to be completed, a Bitcoin transaction needs only two people, each with a wallet, which is a freely downloadable app. As wires are tied to bank accounts, they exclude the estimated 1.7 billion "unbanked" people worldwide who do not have a bank account or similar. A wire may be completed in minutes or hours, but only on non-holiday weekdays and during business hours. Bitcoin can be used at any time. Usually, wires are more expensive than using the Bitcoin network.

Instead of wire, there are Automated Clearing House (ACH) transactions. But they, too, are electronic interbank mechanisms. Therefore, they also require the sender and receiver to have bank accounts; they, too, operate on non-holidays and during business hours. The advantage of ACH over wires is that they are a lower fee, reversible, and enable auto-pay. The disadvantage is that transaction speeds are lower, as ACH transfers can take days versus minutes or hours. In most of these criteria, Bitcoin is advantageous to ACH, except regarding fees.

Credit cards are more flexible than wires or ACH transfers. They do not necessarily presuppose baking access for the sender and receiver – although, in practice, often it is a requirement. Also, credit card transactions can take place anytime. However, credit cards typically charge high fees to the sender and receiver, and the payment takes several days to complete. Credit cards have one advantage over Bitcoin: their fail-safe mechanism to reverse payments, for example, in fraud cases.

Digital payment networks – such as PayPal – are yet another competitor to Bitcoin. Their users do not necessarily need bank accounts. Also, payments can take place at any time. Transactions are seemingly instantaneous, as the network's sponsor – the platform – is effectively reassigning values from one account to another within the platform's private ledger. However, moving money off the platform typically takes a few days. Within the platform, the principle of decentralization works. However, there is the sponsor, which is one entity with which users must interact and which users must trust. Finally, their fees can be lower or higher than Bitcoin's.

Bitcoin transactions are, in most cases, faster and cheaper than off-blockchain or traditional payment methods, as they do not require the involvement of banks or other intermediaries. The lack of a counterparty makes Bitcoin a more efficient way to transfer value, especially for international transactions. Payments can occur at any time of day involving anyone using the internet. Anyone can access the network, even the unbanked population. As a decentralized network, the system is robust, resilient, and safe and does not depend on a central agent.

3.5 Ethereum

Ethereum is a public blockchain launched in 2015. It is a decentralized, open-source platform enabling the building and development of decentralized applications, dapps, and smart contracts securely and efficiently. Presently, most applications are operating in the financial sector, such as marketplaces, exchanges, lending, or derivatives. Increasingly, dapps are being expanded into other sectors, too.

Decentralized applications, dapps, operate autonomously, using smart contracts, running on a distributed ledger system. Dapps operate without human intervention and are (usually) not owned by any entity. Dapps are themselves distributed or determined by the blockchain on which they rely.

Ethereum is a base technology with which decentralized autonomous organizations DAOs, blockchain-based organizations owned and governed by their members, can set up rules and let these be executed by code.

The Ethereum blockchain has a native coin called Ether ETH. It is the intrinsic token known to the Ethereum blockchain and accounts on Ethereum have ether balances maintained in ether. Ether has many use cases on Ethereum. The two most prominent are similar to bitcoin: Ether is a token – digital cash – used for payment between peers, and ether is used to incentivize validators to maintain the blockchain. As in the case of Bitcoin, validators are rewarded when they add information to the distributed ledger. Additionally, they might be tipped. Tipping incentivizes the validator to include a transaction in the next Ethereum block.

Ether's most important use is facilitating the execution of smart contracts and dapps on its native network, Ethereum. This is referred to as gas. Gas is a unit of measurement. It measures the computational effort required to execute transactions or smart contracts. Gas is, therefore, the fee required to conduct an operation on Ethereum. Gas is dynamic and determined on a per-block basis, depending on the complexity of the process and market demand.

In addition to ether, the network's native token, several non-natives are deployed as smart contracts running on Ethereum's base technology. For them, there are two standards:

- ERC-20 is a standard for fungible tokens, for example, stablecoins – tokens that have values pegged to other assets, most commonly the US-Dollar; wrapped tokens – tokens that essentially swap one token for another token in an equal amount via a smart contract; a dapp tokens: tokens used for running dapps, coming with voting rights to govern the dapp and value accrual mechanisms, such as participating in the fees or revenue generated by the dapp.
- ERC-721 is a token standard for non-fungible tokens NFTs on Ethereum. It allows creators to issue unique crypto assets like NFTs via smart contracts. Examples of ERC-721 tokens include digital art NFTs in collections like the Bored Ape Yacht Club and Cryptopunks, as well as domain name NFTs like coinbase.eth. Similar to internet domain names, these .eth name, agents are used to create decentralized websites and to simplify wallet addresses / public keys.

How does the Ethereum blockchain work? Ethereum runs the Ethereum Virtual Machine EVM, a potent global computer storing data and executing code in smart contracts. The EVM is "Turing complete," meaning it can take a program, run it, and find a result. The EVM was designed to be user-friendly and accessible to many developers, regardless of their technical expertise or background. It is relatively easy to use, with a high-level Solidity programming language and a simple, intuitive development environment.

Ethereum's consensus mechanism was PoW for most of its life, similar to Bitcoin's. On September 15, 2022, Ethereum switched to a PoS consensus mechanism to improve energy efficiency and scalability.

In a PoS system, validators produce blocks. Validators stake the native token of the blockchain, in this case, ether. Staking involves locking up the ether in a smart contract. Validators are selected randomly to produce blocks, but the more ether a validator has staked, the more likely they will be chosen. When a validator makes a block, they receive a reward. They can also be tipped by a participant in the network, thus increasing the probability of being selected. If a validator proposes a bad block with invalid transactions, they are at risk of their staked ether being slashed or taken away.

Ethereum's switch to PoS was motivated by increasing the scalability of the network. Proof of Work consensus mechanisms can be slow and resource-intensive, limiting the number of transactions processed per second. Proof of Stake consensus mechanisms are generally faster and more efficient, which could improve the scalability of the Ethereum network, especially when paired with additional planned upgrades over time.

Additionally, in PoS networks, validators are aligned with token holders since they must acquire tokens to be block producers. Compare this to PoW miners, who have no obligation to hold the blockchain's native token. Validators are stakeholders of the network.

A drawback to PoS is the potential for increased centralization, as it is easier to acquire control of block production by purchasing the blockchain's native tokens. Compare that to PoW, where making up most of the network's computing power can be relatively hard and expensive, especially for more mature and competitive blockchains like Bitcoin and Ethereum.

What is the value proposition of Ethereum? It solves several real-world problems. Smart contracts, used to deploy dapps, are this blockchain's most important innovation. They have the potential to be more dynamic than usual contracts and to operate at a lower cost. Both are achieved by eliminating intermediaries.

Some of the most popular dapps are decentralized finance, DeFi, service applications. Decentralized finance aims to use blockchain technology to disrupt traditional financial services. The DeFi applications enable users to access several financial services, for example, lending, borrowing, and trading, in a decentralized and secure manner.

In the DeFi ecosystem on Ethereum, there are many stablecoins. Stablecoins are fungible tokens without or with only minimal volatility. They achieve this by being pegged to a real-world value, such as the US-Dollar or gold.

Ethereum's open and permissionless nature allows any agent connected to the web to participate in its ecosystem. These characteristics enable unbanked agents to participate in financial activities, like sending and receiving money, accessing loans, or investing.

Ethereum has also been used as the basis for NFTs, which create a wide range of unique digital assets, including art, music, and collectibles. Finally, Ethereum has been used as the basis for DAOs. The DAOs have the potential to revolutionize the way that organizations are structured and operate.

Ethereum is one of many use cases for a base technology. Solana, Cardano, Polkadot, Avalance, and Algorand are examples of distributed ledgers emulating Ethereum's use cases and technology. However, Bitcoin, which is focused on transactions, and Ethereum, as a scalable technology, still dominate the digital asset space.

3.6 Payments, Stablecoins

CAIA sees four clusters of digital assets' use cases, the first being payment. Bitcoin and ether – only one of the many functions of the Ethereum blockchain – are such use cases. Other use cases are stablecoins, that is, electronic currencies with a stable value. The value-add of this cluster is straightforward: peers can directly pay each other without the need for an intermediary.

Peer-to-peer payment increases financial inclusion by extending electronic payment options to unbanked agents. It also diminishes transaction costs by eliminating third-party operations, which should translate into lower fees. Finally, it increases the security of the participants because they own a token – instead of having a claim on an accounting entry – and the network is robust and resilient.

Cryptocurrency, as a technical term, comes from the inception of distributed ledger technology to establish a payment system. Bitcoin is so dominant in this space that other coins, including ether, are broadly denominated altcoins, that is, alternatives to Bitcoin.

Stablecoins are a unique category of cryptocurrencies designed to minimize price volatility and maintain a stable value. While traditional cryptocurrencies like Bitcoin and Ether can experience significant price fluctuations, stablecoins aim to provide a reliable unit of account and a medium of exchange for transactions.

How do stablecoins work? Stablecoins are cryptocurrencies. Their design maintains their stable value. They are pegged to a value outside their blockchain to achieve this. This value serves as collateral. Usually, stablecoins need over-collateralization to maintain their stable value. Over-collateralization provides collateral worth more than enough to cover potential losses in drawdown (or default) cases.

Stablecoins aim to reduce price volatility, making them more suitable for everyday transactions. Broadly, there are four different stabilization mechanisms or pegs:

- Fiat-Collateralized Stablecoins: These stablecoins are backed by fiat currency reserves, such as the US Dollar, held in bank accounts. For each stablecoin issued, an equivalent amount of fiat currency is kept in reserve, ensuring the stablecoin's value is linked to the underlying fiat currency. Most stablecoins are pegged to the US-Dollar; examples are Tether USDT, USD Coin USDC, and TrueUSD TUSD.
- Crypto-Collateralized Stablecoins: These stablecoins are backed by other cryptocurrencies held in reserve. To maintain price stability, the value of the reserve cryptocurrencies must exceed the total supply of stablecoins issued. In the event of significant price fluctuations, additional collateral might be required to maintain the stablecoin's peg. Examples of crypto-collateralized stablecoins include MakerDao's DAI, backed by a surplus of Ethereum in a smart contract.
- Physical assets back commodity-backed stablecoins: Natural resources or real estate are examples of such assets. Examples are Tether Gold XAUT and Paxos Gold PAXG.
- Algorithmic Stablecoins: Algorithmic stablecoins are not backed by reserves. Instead, their stability is achieved through algorithmic mechanisms that adjust the stablecoin's supply based on market demand and conditions. These stablecoins often use smart contracts to increase or decrease the supply in response to price changes. Ampleforth AMPL, for example, is an algorithmic stablecoin.

What is the value proposition of stablecoins? With their function being easing payments, stablecoins focus on the interaction between the digital and non-digital spaces, mainly:

- Remittances: Stablecoins offer a faster and more cost-effective alternative for cross-border remittances than traditional banking methods. Using stablecoins allows users to send funds internationally with reduced transaction fees and shorter processing times.
- Merchant Payments: Stablecoins can serve as an efficient means of payment for merchants, providing a stable value for goods and services without worrying about the price volatility often associated with other cryptocurrencies. This stability makes them more appealing for daily transactions.

- Decentralized Finance DeFi Applications: Stablecoins enable users to participate in lending, borrowing, yield farming, and other financial activities with reduced exposure to price fluctuations.
- Financial Inclusion: Stablecoins have the potential to provide access to financial services to individuals in regions with unstable local currencies or limited banking infrastructure. Users can store and transfer value in a more reliable and accessible form.

Despite the advantages of stablecoins, they are not without challenges. Maintaining a stable value requires effective collateral management and, in some cases, audits to ensure adequate backing. Additionally, regulatory scrutiny and concerns about the centralization of reserves have been raised within the stablecoin space.

Another case in the payments cluster is Central Bank Digital Currencies CBDCs. They are digital forms of cash issued by a central bank and are typically pegged to the value of the country's fiat currency. In other words, they are an example of a fiat-backed stablecoin. While digital payments are already a reality with everyday tools like Apple Pay and Square, CBDCs aim to be a more efficient tool by delivering the same experience at a fraction of the cost. On the other hand, none of the core ideas of digital assets – decentralization and trustlessness – are present in CBDCs.

3.7 Decentralized Finance

Decentralized finance, often called DeFi, is a rapidly growing ecosystem of financial applications and services built on blockchain networks. The DeFi creates an open, transparent, and permissionless alternative to traditional financial systems, where users can deploy extensive financial services without intermediaries like banks or financial institutions. Decentralized financial offerings will allow individuals to initiate contracts, collateralize assets, and earn incentives as owners of the networks they use most often.

Decentralized finance operates on decentralized blockchain platforms using smart contracts. These are self-executing contracts. The terms are directly coded into the contract's software. Smart contracts enable automation and transparency; they eliminate the need for intermediaries.

Decentralized finance platforms are open to any agent with access to the web and do not require users to go through traditional Know Your Customer KYC or anti-money laundering AML processes. This openness allows users worldwide to access financial services regardless of location or background. Many DeFi protocols are designed to be interoperable, meaning they can interact with other DeFi applications and assets, creating a seamless and interconnected financial ecosystem.

How does DeFi work? Functionality and governance are critical parts of any specific DeFi application. On the level of technology, most dapps are built on a decentralized blockchain that operates autonomously using smart contracts. Their governance is usually a decentralized autonomous organization DAO.

A DAO has no central authority constructed by rules encoded in digital on-chain and smart contracts. It is controlled by the organization's native token holders, known as members.

The DAOs govern as a collective group by participating and managing the entity. The rules of their governance process are encoded in the underlying smart contracts to incentivize them to act in the entity's best interest. Members collectively decide a DAO's objectives. Forums give users a voice, and proposals offer the power to influence other members. Collectively, the group is in charge.

Transparency is a crucial tenet of DAOs, and not only regarding decision-making. If desired, an investor could retrieve all financial information with only a few lines of computer code, often provided by simple software tools. Examples of DAOs are MakerDAO, Unsiwap, BitDAO, and Aragon.

What is the value proposition of DeFi? DeFi can be applied to any financial contract. Widely used use cases are:

- Liquidity Pools and Automated Market Makers AMMs: DeFi platforms use liquidity pools and automated market maker algorithms to facilitate trading and liquidity provision. Users can add their assets to liquidity pools and earn rewards for providing liquidity, enabling decentralized trading, and reducing reliance on centralized exchanges.

- Lending and Borrowing: DeFi platforms offer decentralized lending and borrowing services, allowing users to lend their digital assets and earn interest or borrow assets against collateral. Smart contracts ensure that loans are automatically executed; their interest rates are determined by supply and demand or by a leading interest rate indicator, as stipulated in the terms.

- Stablecoins: Stablecoins play a crucial role in DeFi by providing a stable value within the ecosystem. They are often used as a medium of exchange and collateral for lending and borrowing activities.

- Yield Farming and Staking: DeFi platforms often reward users for participating in various activities through yield farming and staking. Yield farmers provide liquidity, lock up their tokens in specific smart contracts, and earn additional tokens as rewards.

- Decentralized Exchanges DEXs: Decentralized exchanges enable users to trade cryptocurrencies directly without an intermediary. DEXs are noncustodial, meaning users retain control of their funds throughout trading.

- Blockchain Oracles: An oracle connects the blockchain to the outside world. Specific decentralized applications need external data, and oracles are the gates through which this information gets on-chain. Prediction markets treat events, like elections, as financial products. Data confirm who predicted the results and releases payouts using smart contracts. Software oracles usually connect to user-friendly applications through publicly available tools. Hardware oracles with physical sensors are used to determine things like wind speed, which can be important for applications like insurance.
- Insurance: Insurance is a popular blockchain and smart contract application. It is well suited for parametric insurance or claims paid to the party involved if specific parameters are met, usually around a well-defined event. Some examples would be weather, farming, and natural disasters. Parametric insurance often uses hardware and software oracles to determine when a payout should occur.
- Derivatives. Like derivatives in traditional markets, DeFi derivatives allow users to interact with assets without owning them directly. Many DeFi derivatives are tied to digital assets but can track traditional ones. Most DeFi derivatives marketplaces enable traders to use leverage to increase their potential returns alongside an increase in risk.

3.8 Tokens

Tokens have already been explained in the previous section, allowing this section to be shortened. They are digital assets that can serve as a medium of exchange for transactions, a store of value, or a way to access certain services or functions on a blockchain or dapp. Tokens are digital "things," that is, units with assigned properties that can be owned – and usually are – by a specific agent.

How do tokens work? They are created and operated on a blockchain platform and often implemented as smart contracts, self-executing contracts with predefined rules written in code. These smart contracts define the behavior of the token. The definition includes how it can be created, transferred, and managed. Some blockchains, like Ethereum, have token standards for exchange.

Token creation typically involves deploying a smart contract with the necessary functionalities for the token. They are usually associated with specific blockchain addresses (wallets). The wallet owner has control over the tokens associated with that address. Wallets are secured using cryptographic keys, and only the owner who possesses the private key can access and manage the tokens in that wallet.

Token transfers occur on the blockchain through transactions. When a token is sent from one wallet to another, a transaction is created and recorded on the blockchain, updating the tokens' ownership.

What is the value proposition of Tokens? Tokens can have various use cases, depending on their design and purpose. Some common use cases include:

- Digital Currency: Tokens can be a digital representation of fiat currency (e.g., stablecoins) or have intrinsic value like cryptocurrencies.
- Utility Tokens: These tokens grant access to services or functionalities within a decentralized application or platform. Utility tokens are associated with an ecosystem of specific crypto platforms. These tokens have defined use cases within the ecosystem and are necessary to participate in the platform. Utility tokens offer functionalities within the platform, such as voting rights, access to premium features, or the ability to exchange goods and services. They are not meant to be investments. For example, a utility token may be used as collateral for a decentralized loan. With the deposit of the utility token, the smart contract providing a loan would be executed. Other examples may be access to exclusive promotions, reduced fees, or other benefits only made available to users of the utility token.
- Security tokens replicate traditional securities like stocks and bonds, with the only difference of them being digital and coded into a blockchain. They represent ownership in a company's stock, giving holders a claim on its profits and assets. Additionally, they can represent ownership of real estate, art, and collectibles. Security tokens offer several benefits compared to traditional methods of owning and trading assets. An agent can buy and sell them quickly and easily using blockchain technology, and they can be easily fractionalized, diving ownership into smaller units to make it easier for agents to buy and sell smaller quantities of an asset.
- Governance Tokens: The holders of governance Tokens play a part in the governance and decision-making processes of a DAO or decentralized protocol. In a decentralized system, governance tokens replace boards of directors and other central authorities.
- NFTs: Non-fungible tokens represent ownership of unique assets, such as digital art, collectibles, virtual real estate, and more.

3.9 WEB 3.0

Web 3.0 is the decentralized web, or the next iteration of the internet, that aims to shift from the current centralized model to a more decentralized and user-centric paradigm. It envisions a future where data, identity, and applications are not controlled by a few centralized entities but are distributed across a network of interconnected nodes, giving users more control over their digital experiences.

Web 3.0 relies on blockchain technology, decentralized protocols, and other emerging technologies to achieve its goals.

In Web 3.0, users have more ownership and control over their data and digital identities. They can manage access to their information and selectively share it with various applications without relying on third-party platforms. Web 3.0 promotes interoperability between applications and platforms, enabling seamless data exchange and interactions. This characteristic allows users to move data and assets across various services and dapps without being locked into specific ecosystems.

How does Web 3.0 work? The fundamental principles are similar to those of digital assets. For this reason, these assets will play an essential role in the development of Web 3.0:

- Decentralization: Web 3.0 emphasizes decentralization, where data and applications are distributed across a network of nodes, reducing reliance on central servers and minimizing single points of failure.
- Blockchain Technology: Blockchain is a foundational technology for Web 3.0. It enables the creation of trustless and tamper-resistant systems, ensuring transparency and immutability of data. Smart contracts, self-executing code on blockchains, significantly automate processes and interactions in Web 3.0 applications.
- Decentralized Applications dapps: Web 3.0 is characterized by decentralized applications that run on blockchain networks or other peer-to-peer protocols. These dapps often leverage smart contracts and are governed by consensus mechanisms rather than centralized authorities.
- Tokenization and Digital Assets: Tokens, such as cryptocurrencies and non-fungible tokens, play a fundamental role in Web 3.0. They represent ownership of digital assets, facilitate economic interactions, and incentivize network participants.
- Privacy and Security: Web 3.0 prioritizes user privacy and security. Since data are not concentrated in a single location, the risk of large-scale data breaches is reduced. Additionally, cryptographic techniques and secure identity systems enhance individual privacy.
- Open-Source Collaboration: Web 3.0 projects embrace open-source principles, encouraging collaboration and community-driven development, which fosters innovation and enables a more inclusive approach to building the decentralized web.
- File and Data Sharing: Users can work collaboratively sharing data and files, for example, in one-company or multicompany networks.

What is the value proposition of digital assets in Web 3.0? As a decentralized and user-centric iteration of the web, Web 3.0 relies on digital assets to function:

- Gaming: In Web 3.0 gaming, players use digital assets to buy and sell in-game items, participate in competitions, and earn rewards transparently and securely. Web3 gaming also allows the creation of non-fungible tokens representing in-game items, characters, or other assets. Decentralized, it changes how players engage in online games – they own their identities and gaming items that can be used elsewhere. Today, users pay for games for the value of experiences provided by game producers. They own nothing but the right to play the game. On the other hand, Web 3.0 gaming can create new business models with new revenue streams for game developers and publishers by allowing them to monetize in-game items and experiences directly.
- Social Media: Web 3.0 social media platforms use digital assets to enable users to buy and sell content, access premium features, and earn rewards for their contributions. They may also use non-fungible tokens to represent unique profiles, posts, or other content. Again, users can monetize their engagements and content. The base layers of the digital ecosystem are fundamental elements. Exchanging money for an NFT in a social media setting is most straightforward with a digital wallet, the Lightning network, or a stablecoin.
- Metaverse: The Metaverse is a shared digital space where an agent can interact with others and digital objects. User experiences are immersive, and main-stream companies are engaged with the Metaverse. Epic Games has developed the "Metaverse Engine," Meta (formerly known as Facebook) is working on its "Horizon" platform, "Project Metaverse" is the creation of IBM, and Sony aims for entertainment through "Project Field." As those virtual worlds expand, so do the services around them. Virtual design, architecture, art, clothing, music, and asset management can reside in the Metaverse.
- Financial Services: Despite decentralization, financial services also have a part to play within Web3. Micro, peer-to-peer transactions will require the adoption of digital wallets. In other words, where there is activity to be monetized, there is a need for financial services. DeFi is a natural service provider in Web 3, but traditional banks also experiment in places like the Metaverse. J.P. Morgan, Standard Chartered, and HSBC have "virtual offices" in the Metaverse.
- Identity Tools: Web3 identity tools manage and verify the identity of individuals and organizations on decentralized platforms. Self-sovereign identity systems allow users to control their digital identity data. Decentralized identity systems store and manage identity data. Verifiable credentials use blockchain and cryptographic tools to validate certificates from a trusted party, like a college diploma or a government driver's license.

- Currency: Like decentralized money, Web3 seeks to increase efficiency, broaden inclusiveness, and lower consumer costs. Most importantly, it aims to give them the power to own and manage their data.

4 Risk and Valuation of Digital Assets

Abstract: A mosaic approach is needed in evaluating a digital asset's risk profile. Digital Assets are a new asset class. They bear risks, and the industry is still searching for adequate valuation methods. The digital asset space lacks established institutional dealers of information, for example, rating agencies or research institutions. Information in and about this pace is often unsystematic, dispersed, or biased. The most significant risks of digital assets are financial, technological, and operational. Several valuation methods exist for evaluating digital assets, chiefly market capitalization and total addressable market, stock-to-flow, and cost of capital, as well as discounted cash flow and multiples.

This section argues that a mosaic approach is needed to evaluate a digital asset's risk profile and determine its economic value. It explores the risks and valuation methods of digital assets. Any investment faces several types of risk. In the case of digital assets, the novelty of the space, its decentralized nature, and its technological pace contribute to its high risks. As the risks are high, so are the opportunities. The valuation of these opportunities can be a challenge. Several methods exist, yet they still need to establish themselves as standard or best in class. This section discusses the following topics:

- An overview of risks
- Financial risks
- Technological risks
- Operational risks
- Valuation methods and tokenomics
- Market capitalization and total addressable market
- Stock-to-Flow and cost-of-production valuation
- Discounted Cash Flow
- Multiples

The first section is a general introduction to risks. These risks can be grouped into three: financial, technological, and operational risks, each discussed in a separate section. There are several valuation methods in tokenomics. They are introduced in a separate section, while the specific methods making up the mosaic approach are explained in a separate section. They are market capitalization, stock-to-flow, discounted cash flow, and multiples.

4.1 An Overview of Risks

Digital assets offer significant opportunities, for example, high returns in payment methods and DeFi, and diversification in stablecoins and tokenization. Digital assets enable experimental approaches like Web 3.0 or increasing efficiency with smart contracts. They thrust governance with DAOs, and they are inclusive of unbanked agents. However, despite their many use cases, they also bear risks.

As alternative investments – following CAIA's viewpoint (CAIA 2023) – the risks of digital assets are either different from those in other asset classes or present themselves in ways that are specific to this asset class and unfamiliar to other asset classes. Understanding and accepting these risks is the first step in deploying strategies to handle them as an investor.

Discussing the risks of digital assets depends on their specific use cases. The risks of payment methods differ from those in DeFi, tokens, or Web 3.0. Contemporarily, there is a focus on the risks and valuation of tokens, also called cryptocurrencies, used in payment systems. Since most payment systems and DeFi rely on tokens, addressing their risks covers those other use cases, at least at a basic level. Web 3.0 is still at its inception, so the research on its risks and valuations will follow as it establishes itself.

Following this approach, this section discusses the risks mainly of cryptocurrencies, first at large, as an overview in this section, and then, in the following sections, in more detail, grouping them into three: financial, technological, and operational. As a starting point, the risks generally associated with digital assets are:

- Lack of information and Misinformation: Digital assets are relatively new. Many market participants have little or no information and practice, or experience in this space. Usual dealers of information, that is, intermediaries and research venues, still need to be solidly established. Moreover, their establishment is rendered difficult by the very proposition of digital assets to function without the need for third parties. Additionally, the digital asset markets are rife with misinformation and unreliable sources.
- Speculation: Many investors in the digital asset space are driven by the potential for quick profits, often with little regard for the asset's underlying technology or long-term prospects. This speculative nature can lead to irrational exuberance and bubbles that eventually burst. The effects of the speculative thrust can be significant in digital assets because of their lack of intrinsic or floor value.
- Value: Digital assets often lack intrinsic value or underlying assets. Instead, supply and demand value them according to their preferences. As a result, market sentiment can significantly impact their prices.

- Price Volatility: Prices can experience rapid and substantial fluctuations within short periods. On the one hand, it creates opportunities for significant gains; on the other hand, it also exposes investors to the risk of substantial losses. Various factors, including regulatory changes, market sentiment, technological developments, and macroeconomic events, can influence sudden market swings.
- Liquidity: Some digital assets, notably smaller and less popular ones, may suffer from low liquidity. Buying or selling significant amounts of these assets can be challenging without causing substantial price fluctuations. Illiquid markets may also make it harder to exit positions quickly during market stress.
- Regulation: In many countries, the regulatory environment for cryptocurrencies and digital assets is still evolving. Governments may introduce new laws or policies impacting the market, trading platforms, or assets. Sudden regulatory changes could lead to price drops, liquidity issues, or even restrictions on trading and ownership.
- Market Manipulation: The digital asset market's relatively young and less regulated nature can expose it to market manipulation. Pump-and-dump schemes, where the price of an asset is artificially inflated and then sold off at a profit, are not uncommon. Investors with limited experience in this space can be particularly vulnerable to such tactics.
- IT-Security: Digital assets are often stored in digital wallets, and the security of these wallets is critical. If you're not careful, you might fall victim to hacking, phishing attacks, or other forms of cybercrime. Exchanges and trading platforms can also be targets for hackers. Losing access to your assets or having them stolen is a real risk.
- IT-Networks: Digital assets rely on blockchain technology and other technological platforms. Issues like network congestion, software bugs, or changes to the underlying technology can disrupt the normal functioning of assets and related services.
- Energy: Some digital assets, notably Bitcoin, need electricity as an input and to run. In some countries, especially in the global north, electricity has become increasingly scarce and costly, negatively impacting the economics of digital assets.
- Fraud: As in any other innovative sector, the lack of transparency and the obsolescence in information attracts fraudulent behavior. There have been many instances of fraud in the digital asset space. Often, these risks go hand in hand with centralization tendencies, for example by having an agent with a high market power or a marketplace with unclear governance.

4.2 Financial Risks

Above, volatility, liquidity, speculation, and intrinsic value are identified as areas with risks for digital assets. From the investor's or portfolio allocator's stance, an additional risk involves the difficulty in **modeling** digital assets. Their risk assessment is by itself complex.

The modeling challenge starts with a lack of transparency. While individual blockchains can be highly transparent, the aggregated asset class is not. Some use cases, such as cryptocurrency, have public data and exposure, but DeFi and Web 3.0 have yet to. Regarding financial risks, cryptocurrencies are often proxies for the whole asset class. But even this proposition is difficult to assess.

To model **returns**, investors and allocators need enough historical data to find samples and phenotypes of behavior. Given the digital assets space's newness, there is little or no historical data. More importantly, new digital assets come into the market without data, often claiming to be uncorrelated from other digital assets.

Bitcoin and Ether have more extended time series. But it is doubtful whether some of their early and bubble returns, such as over 1,000 percent gains in months, can be replicated as they mature. On the other hand, even with their maturation, volatility remains an issue complicating any modeling.

Finally, since the number of digital assets held and run by institutional investors is still being determined, it is also challenging to assess the asset class's relevance in professionally managed portfolios. The reports on returns broadcasted to the public might be neither representative nor reliable for the professional investment space.

The **volatility** and the drawdown of digital assets are often identified as their primary financial risk. With the time series for the longer-lived crypto assets, one could calculate different risk measures, such as the value at risk or the conditional value at risk. But then, the specifics of digital assets strike again. These measures are only suitable for tokens and payment systems. They cannot be applied to DeFi or Web 3.0.

Also, each crypto asset has its pattern. The average daily volatility in 2021 of Solana and Ripple is 8 percent; Ether shows 6 percent, and Bitcoin 4 percent (CAIA 2023). Most of them have an asymmetric exposure to shocks. Positive shocks affect Bitcoin more strongly than negative ones, while it is the reverse for many other tokens. Ether seems to have become neutral to shocks since 2020 (Schneider 2023).

Academic research suggests that heavy tail distributions, that is, approach zero asymptotically but at a slower rate and can have outliers with very high values, better fitting the cryptocurrencies' characteristics. Also, most cryptos are skewed but with no generalizable pattern, whether to the right or the left of a normal distribution.

At first sight, the market for most cryptocurrencies is liquid. They can be traded any day and around the clock, and most of their trading places are decentralized. **Illiquidity** has, however, been a problem for several digital assets. For example, during the ICO boom of 2017 and 2018, many new cryptocurrencies were launched through fundraising events known as initial coin offerings ICO. Some of these ICO tokens faced significant illiquidity issues after fundraising. Investors found trading these tokens on exchanges challenging, leading to reduced liquidity and difficulty in exiting positions.

Many altcoins, especially those with low market capitalization and smaller communities, have experienced periods of illiquidity. Thin order books and low trading volumes can cause substantial price fluctuations, making it difficult for traders and investors to execute orders at desired prices. Cryptocurrencies that fail to maintain sufficient liquidity or face regulatory issues may be delisted from larger exchanges.

While illiquidity risks exist in the cryptocurrency space, the transparent nature of most blockchains provides a suitable means for assessing it. When using a public blockchain, all transactions are known. Most notably, information on active addresses, wallets, and daily active users is available. Coins and tokens exhibiting greater liquidity are typically associated with more significant numbers of active addresses and daily active users.

Another example of liquidity risk is centralized services freezing user accounts, which is a particularly acute risk with centralized exchanges and businesses offering DeFi-style services. Additionally, some exchanges have been shut down, either for political reasons (mainly in China) or because they are fraudulent. The shutdown of an exchange stops the trade of a crypto asset, leading it into illiquidity.

An essential feature of blockchain technology is the elimination of **counterparty risk**. Decentralized systems are not reliant on any one individual or organization. As the digital asset ecosystem has grown, there has been an influx of centralized services intended to support, complement, and enhance the underlying technologies. The addition of these centralized services reintroduces counterparty risk, such as:

- Centralized Exchanges: Most cryptocurrency trading occurs on centralized exchanges. When agents deposit their cryptocurrencies on a centralized exchange, they trust the exchange with custody of their funds. The agent loses their holdings if the exchange suffers a security breach or becomes insolvent.

- Custodial Wallets: Many users store their cryptocurrencies in custodial wallets provided by third-party service providers. By doing so, they trust the custodian to keep their assets secure. If the custodian experiences a security breach or mismanagement of funds, it can result in user losses.
- Over-the-Counter OTC Trading: In OTC trading, parties transact directly with each other, often facilitated by brokers or intermediaries. If one party fails to honor their side of the agreement, the other party could be at risk of financial loss.
- Smart contract as a counterparty: Smart contracts can have bugs or vulnerabilities that malicious actors could exploit. If a smart contract is flawed, it could have unintended consequences and even loss of funds.
- Token Issuers and ICOs: Investing in tokens issued through ICOs or token sales carries counterparty risk. Investors may suffer financial losses if the issuing entity fails to deliver on its promises or the project does not materialize as expected.
- DeFi Platforms: While DeFi platforms aim to eliminate intermediaries, they can still involve counterparty risk. Users may deposit their cryptocurrencies into smart contracts to participate in various financial activities, and if the smart contract has vulnerabilities or is exploited, funds could be lost.

Users may only sometimes realize whether their service is centralized or decentralized. The industry has several examples of users believing their coins or tokens are being held in segregated wallets only to discover the assets were commingled in an account owned by the centralized service provider.

4.3 Technological Risks

The digital asset space consists of codes or algorithms. As such, the usual IT-related technological risks do exist. Bugs or errors may result in unintended consequences, and cybercrime is nothing new to the world of technology.

Despite using cryptography to enhance overall security, cryptocurrency users are vulnerable to **hackers**. One common target is private key information held in wallets. Given the irreversibility of transactions, should a hacker obtain a private key, they could immediately transfer the digital assets to a wallet controlled by the hacker. In addition to moving coins, cybercriminals also target NFTs and other digital assets of value controlled by private keys/wallets.

Obsolescence is another technological risk. New blockchains, Layer 2 solutions, and other services enter the market regularly, promising improvements over existing technologies. The faster, safer, and cheaper prospects threaten incumbent digital asset technologies. While existing systems can be and are upgraded, there is no guarantee they will not lose out to newer entrants featuring superior technology and ultimately become abandoned blockchains with value-less coins.

The **choice of blockchain** and **governance** is the most critical techno-logical risk. Blockchains can be either public or private. In the case of private blockchains, the operator typically maintains control of the block-chain, meaning it is intermediated. While many users associate digital assets with decentralization and disintermediation, many services in the digital asset ecosystem are operated by one entity or a small group. In those, rules can be changed instantly, assets seized or lost, and services shut down or changed.

However, operating as a public, decentralized blockchain or service is not enough to eliminate governance risks. Systems with governance tokens may have a concentration of ownership, such that a few users control most of the tokens and significantly influence outcomes.

A PoW blockchain could be controlled by a cohort of miners that contribute more than 50 percent of the network power or be the aim of an attack taking over the 51 percent. Just because something exists in the digital asset ecosys-tem does not mean it is decentralized and free of intermediaries or controlling parties.

One crucial rule in the protocol is the number of coins associated with the blockchain. The cap, if any, on the total number of coins and the pace of new issuance varies from one blockchain to the next. Protocols without caps or with high volumes of issuance are at greater risk for devaluation from the dilution in supply. To combat this risk, some protocols (for example, Ethereum) include a feature that "burns" supply, that is, permanently removing coins, to keep issuance and volume in check.

In addition to these risks, the **blockchain trilemma** persists. A trade-off for many blockchains is scale, typically at the expense of decentralization.

Each blockchain is a **unique technology** with a specified coin for use on that blockchain. To operate the Bitcoin blockchain, the agent must use Bitcoin. To run the Ethereum blockchain, the user must use Ether. Each blockchain is independent; therefore, if users wish to participate across multiple blockchains, they must hold the coins of each blockchain.

Layer 2 solutions exist to reduce this friction; however, these solutions may bring their risks. Most famously, a layer two solution called Wormhole was designed to allow users to use a cryptocurrency from one blockchain to make trades and purchases on another. In February 2022, this service was hacked, and over 300 million US-Dollars in Ethereum were stolen. According to cryptocur-rency insiders, interoperability solutions lost nearly 2 billion US-Dollars in user funds in 2022.

4.4 Operational Risks

There are several sub-types of operational risks of digital assets. The most significant are:

- Regulation is a risk because it can constrict the digital assets' space, impose new costs, constrain decentralization, and generally throttle new or current investment ideas. It should be remembered: Digital assets were designed to operate partially outside of the regulated realm and even emerge as competition to regulations and jurisdictions.
- Energy intensity: Digital assets need energy to run. Some, like Bitcoin, need electricity as an input. However, energy is becoming scarcer and more costly. If investors and portfolio aggregators are preoccupied with ESG – Environmental, Social, and Governance – not only the energy consumption of digital assets but also the primary source of energy production and its alternate uses become a risk.
- Fraud can happen in any space. In the digital assets' ecosystem, it can come from fraudulent websites or apps, fake investment schemes, or fraudulent liquidity mining platforms. The pump and dump scheme is a very problematic fraud case – not unique to this space. Scammers identify a coin or token to promote to the vulnerable audience. The scammers will hold the coin before the promotion and may use internal funds following the promotion to pump up volume and price to entice outside investment. As the victims begin investing and furthering the price action, the scammers sell their holdings and take profit, leaving the victims holding a coin with a price well above intrinsic value destined to fall once liquidity or volume normalizes.
- Loss of Identifier: Digital assets typically use public and private keys to transact, but especially to guarantee a user's ownership over a token or any other digital asset. Users "store" their assets in wallets. There are several types of wallets with different value propositions. Users investing in this space will typically need to use many wallets simultaneously, adding some complexity to the operations of digital assets. For example, some wallets are hot, that is, connected to the internet. They can be hacked, misused, or misplaced. Some wallets can be cold, that is, disconnected from the internet, for example, stored in a thumb drive. They can be lost or broken. Since the private key is private and, in most cases, not duplicable, the user severs their connection to the digital asset once they are lost.

4.5 Valuation Methods and Tokenomics

The discussion about risks focused on tokens, or cryptocurrencies, because they are, on a basic level, the operating paradigm of most digital assets. Similarly, the explanation of valuation methods puts the token in its center, assuming that the value of a digital asset is intrinsically intertwined with the token it uses.

Note that this is a simplification. This intrinsic connection might be the case in payment systems and some DeFi. However, most applications of DeFi do not have the token at the core of their value proposition but the decentralization and automation of contract relationships. If they use a coin, it has a facilitating, not a constitutive, function. The valuation of these business models should take the value added by the DeFi contract itself as a value driver. While it is still industry standard to conduct valuation via tokens, the valuation of DeFi on its terms is rapidly evolving.

Generally, market capitalization and total addressable market methods can be applied to any digital asset. Stock-to-flow and cost-of-production metrics are suited for PoW tokens. Discounted Cash Flows and Multiples fit revenue or cash flow generating PoS tokens or DeFi.

Often, traditional valuation methods do not apply to digital assets. They are intangible and do not generate cash flows like equity and debt. Also, this space's new and evolving character imposes additional challenges to valuation methods. Nonetheless, agents can better understand a specific digital asset's value by applying different valuation methods. Using several methods simultaneously is a variation of a mosaic approach. While none can give a complete picture, their combination can convey a general image of the fair value range.

Before taking a closer look at different methods, it is worthwhile discussing "**tokenomics**." It refers to a digital asset's common and unique elements that make it valuable. Network effects are common to all tokens. The effect relates the number of users of a token to its value. Hence, the more users, the higher value. The operationalization of this effect occurs through several different functions.

Metcalfe's law is one of them. In tokenomics, this law says that a network's value is the square of the number of its nodes. The formula for Metcalfe's Law is $n*(n-1)/2$. The small n is the number of users in a network. For blockchains, there are a few ways to define users. One that is most used in this context is the number of wallets, or addresses, representing the network of end users holding digital assets that can be exchanged with others on the network.

A simple application of Metcalfe's Law by CAIA regresses the value of Bitcoin against the number of Bitcoin addresses as a proxy for users in a historical timeline. A strongly positive relationship exists with the regression function explaining 91 percent of the data.

According to CAIA (CAIA 2023), there are five key metrics in tokenomics:

- Token supply, whereby there is a difference in maximum supply or any cap a token might have in-built, and circulating supply, the number of tokens in circulation.

- Token Utility is the token's use case, as referred to in Section 3 of this Element.
- Token Distribution refers to how tokens are brought into the market. A fair launch involves launching tokens without any prior access or private allocations. A pre-mining launch distributes tokens privately before they are released to the public. Additionally, agents should consider the distribution methods, the timing of distribution, lockups, and release schedules.
- Token Retirement or "Burns" take a certain number of tokens permanently out of circulation, making them unusable and reducing their total supply. This action is typically performed by sending the tokens to a wallet address from which they cannot be accessed or spent.
- Token incentive Mechanisms are the elements of blockchain governance that induce agents to maintain the distributed ledger. Such mechanisms include mining, staking, decision-making, network benefits, and, if applicable, bonuses.

4.6 Market Capitalization and Total Addressable Market

These two methods focus on the market as the initial place to look for information. The comparison of the market with the algorithm produces a value.

Market capitalization is a simple valuation method that multiplies the current price of a digital asset by its total circulating supply. It gives an estimate of the total value of all units of the asset in circulation. Market cap is widely used to compare the relative size of different cryptocurrencies and is often considered for established assets like Bitcoin and Ethereum.

Similarly, token utility and adoption metrics can match market prices, leading to capitalization. For utility tokens, assessing the level of adoption and usage of the token within the associated platform or ecosystem can be valuable. Metrics like the number of active addresses, daily transactions, and developer activity on the blockchain can provide insights into the token's value. In the case of a new market, an analogy based on an existing market can be built.

Total Addressable Market (TAM) evaluates a token's growth potential by comparing market universes. For example, suppose the total global household wealth is 200 trillion dollars, and the supply of Bitcoin is capped at 21 million coins. In that case, the value of one Bitcoin is around 10 million dollars. BTC has significant growth potential compared to its contemporary trading value of below 70,000 dollars per Bitcoin.

At first sight, this number seems unrealistic. However, this admittedly crude method is not only producing a number but also about indicating a tendency. The tendency of the Bitcoin example is that there is more upside (10 million to 50,000 US-Dollars) than downside (50,000 to 0) for investing in BTC.

There are more refined versions of TAM. One way of refining it is to segment the market and identify market shares for a given token in each segment. For example, there are around 120 million tokens of Ether in circulation. The total volume of the gold market is 5.5 trillion US-Dollars. Say, 10 percent of ETH is used to take a market share of 5 percent of gold. The total volume of the real estate market is 200 trillion; 30 percent of ETH is used to take a market share of 15 percent of real estate. Defining segments of addressable markets and the market share of the token in each segment leads to a total value across segments of 800,000 Us-Dollars per Ether.

Again, it is not the numeric value that interests here but the tendency. This refined version of TAM leads to a more granular view of how the token becomes valuable by fulfilling its primary function according to its use case. But the result, the value of Ether, is a number. It can be compared to its contemporary market value of around 2,000 US-Dollars, indicating more upside than downside.

4.7 Stock-to-Flow and Cost-of-Production

The core idea of these methods is to reflect the scarcity constraints of a token on its value. Stock-to-flow methods establish a relationship between the times it would take to replenish the token if its blockchain was to start over. The longer it takes, the scarcer the token and the higher its potential value. According to the cost-of-production method, scarcity depends on how much input, for example, proof of work, is needed to produce one unit of output, the token. Both these methods go back to the valuation of natural assets.

The **stock-to-flow** valuation method analyses the relationship between "stock" and "flow." Stock refers to the total supply of a token at a given time. Flow is the production rate of new tokens. The model's value for digital assets is found by dividing the circulating supply of coins by the annualized issuance of the coin.

The higher an asset's stock-to-flow ratio, the more valuable it should be because assets with a high stock-to-flow ratio are considered scarcer and should command a higher price.

The stock-to-flow model has been used to value Bitcoin because it has a limited supply of 21 million units and a predictable production rate. The amount of new bitcoin that enters circulation over a given period can be considered bitcoin's inflation. The model suggests that as the stock of bitcoin grows and the flow of new bitcoins slows, the value of bitcoin should increase.

For example, if at a certain point in time, the yearly issuance of Bitcoin is 400,000 tokens against its total circulation of 19 million coins, the stock-to-flow ratio of BTC is 47.5. If, at a later point in time, the parameters change to 20 million coins in circulation and 300,000 tokens being supplied yearly, the ratio becomes 66.67, indicating more scarcity and a higher value of BTC. In practice, this value will increase after the next bitcoin halving event in 2024, when the number of new bitcoins released per block will decrease by half.

This method, however, has drawbacks: It does not factor in any market sentiment or exogenous developments, such as political, regulatory, or economic factors. Also, it does not account for changes within the blockchain itself. Most importantly, it cannot be applied to several tokens since it is designed for and applied to assets with a fixed or limited supply and a predictable emission rate. Also, it is questionable how this model should accurately predict the value of tokens with stable, such as Ripple XPR, or negative issuance, such as Ether.

The **cost-of-production** method is a valuation approach used to determine the intrinsic value of tokens. It is based on the idea that there is a link between the value of a token and the cost of its production. This method is more commonly applied to mined cryptocurrencies, like Bitcoin and others that use PoW. The outcome of the valuation is a natural floor value for the token.

For example, valuing Bitcoin using the cost of production model includes identifying the cost of the electricity and other resources used to power the miners' computers to solve the cryptographic puzzles required for validating transactions, which is to add new blocks to the Bitcoin blockchain and earn Bitcoin.

A theory for why mining costs should equal bitcoin's price is that more miners will join the network when mining costs are lower than bitcoin's market value. When mining costs exceed a miner's revenue, the number of miners will decrease.

This approach is well suited for tokens in which the difficulty of work changes dynamically. For example, mining difficulty, a parameter that adjusts over time in many PoW cryptocurrencies, can affect the profitability of mining. As mining difficulty increases, producing new tokens becomes more expensive and resource-intensive, potentially impacting the token's intrinsic value.

The cost-of-production method is limited, mainly when applied to cryptocurrencies with different consensus mechanisms (e.g., proof-of-stake) or pre-mined supply. It may not fully account for factors influencing token value, such as utility, network effects, technological advancements, and market sentiment.

4.8 Discounted Cash Flows

Discounted Cash Flow DCF analysis attempts to estimate the present value of future cash flows generated by a digital asset. It requires assumptions about revenue generation, growth rates, and discount rates. The DCF is commonly used for projects with predictable cash flows, such as DeFi platforms.

The DCF analysis adds up the present value of a company's future cash flows. Usually, it involves the following steps:

- Estimate Cash Flows: Determine the expected future cash flows generated by the digital asset. For cryptocurrencies, these cash flows may come from various sources, such as transaction fees (for blockchain-based platforms), staking rewards (for proof-of-stake assets), or utility token fees (for decentralized applications).
- Project Future Cash Flows: Forecast the future cash flows over a specific time horizon. One can rely on historical data, market trends, adoption rates, technological developments, and other relevant factors to set up this projection. Cryptocurrencies can be highly volatile, so conservative and realistic assumptions are crucial.
- Determine the Discount Rate: Choose an appropriate discount rate to return future cash flows to their present value. The discount rate represents the risk associated with the investment and the opportunity cost of capital. For cryptocurrencies, the discount rate might be adjusted to account for traditional assets' higher risk and volatility. Currently, these rates are in the range of 12–15 percent per year.
- Calculate Present Value: Use the projected future cash flows and the discount rate to calculate the present value of each cash flow, dividing each cash flow by (1 + discount rate) raised to the power of the corresponding year.
- Sum Present Values: Sum up the present values of all future cash flows to get the total present value of the digital asset.
- Consider Terminal Value: In some cases, the DCF analysis may include a terminal value to account for cash flows beyond the projected time horizon. This value is estimated using a suitable multiple or perpetual growth rate.
- Perform Sensitivity Analysis: Given the uncertainties in the cryptocurrency market, perform sensitivity analysis to evaluate how changes in key assumptions, such as growth or discount rates, might impact the valuation.

Take Ethereum as an example: Ethereum charges fees to those who use block space on the network. These fees can serve as top-line revenue in the DCF model. On the other hand, Ethereum rewards network validators who provide security and production of blocks. In a complete simplification of the model, when demand for block space exceeds the rewards paid to validators to produce blocks, Ethereum buys back (burns) more tokens than it pays in expenses. Thus, the network operates at a profit.

In the case of a dapp, frequently, they charge users fees for the services their app provides. These fees can serve as revenues in the DCF. Expenses can include costs of further developing the dapp. For example, a DAO pays contributors for their work on enhancements to the Dapps's protocol. Expenses can also include diluting the dapp's token to incentivize behavior on the dapp or to bring new users to the dapp. Here are two examples:

- Ethereum Name Service ENS is a domain name registry protocol built using the Ethereum blockchain. It allows the registration of any .eth domain, such as hello.eth. Its use cases are manifold, for example, human-readable wallet addresses, decentralized websites, and email addresses. Revenues: ENS charges an annual fee to register domains, a proxy for ENS's revenues. By applying growth expectations to the number of domains registered for the next ten years, an agent can calculate expected ENS revenue by year. Expenses: There are costs of further developing the ENS protocol. They are paid through grants from the ENS treasury. These are ENS's expenses.
- Lido is a noncustodial liquid staking solution for Ethereum and other PoS blockchains. The dapp allows users to stake their Ether with validators without locking up their assets or maintaining staking infrastructure. Revenues: Lido takes 5 percent of the staking rewards generated for users who stake their tokens with Lido validators. Expenses: Lido has an ecosystem grants organization that distributes capital to maintain the Lido ecosystem. Historically, one of the largest spending categories was on security assessments and audits to test Lido's smart contracts. Another expense type was token incentives that are expended to help Lido grow on other blockchain networks.

4.9 Multiples

Multiples is a standard valuation method in traditional finance. Multiples compare a financial metric of revenue or cash-generating digital asset to a similar metric of comparable assets or benchmarks. Metrics could be:

- Price-to-Earnings P/E Ratio: The P/E ratio compares the current market price of a crypto asset to its earnings (or profits) per token. In traditional finance, a low P/E ratio may indicate an undervalued asset, while a high P/E ratio may suggest an overvalued asset. However, P/E ratios are less commonly used in crypto, as many crypto assets are not profit-generating or have variable earnings.
- Price-to-Sales P/S Ratio: The P/S ratio compares the market price of a digital asset to its revenue per token. This ratio can be more relevant for

digital assets, especially for projects that generate revenue through transaction fees or other sources. A lower P/S ratio implies that the asset is undervalued compared to its revenue-generating potential.

- Market Cap-to-Total Value Locked TVL Ratio: For DeFi projects, the Market Cap-to-TVL ratio compares the project's market capitalization to the total value of assets locked in the project's smart contracts. This ratio can provide insights into how the market values the project's capabilities and user base.
- Network Value-to-Transactions NVT Ratio: The NVT ratio divides a digital asset's market capitalization by its daily transaction volume. It helps assess the asset's valuation relative to the economic activity happening on its network. A lower NVT ratio might suggest that the asset is undervalued compared to its utility and adoption.
- Token Price-to-Earnings Growth PEG Ratio: The PEG ratio adjusts the P/E ratio by incorporating the expected earnings growth rate of the asset. This metric can provide a more comprehensive view of the asset's valuation by considering its growth potential and current earnings.
- Token Velocity: Token velocity measures the rate at which tokens change hands on the network. A lower token velocity might indicate that the asset is being held for long-term investment or utility purposes, potentially suggesting higher value or scarcity.

Here is a constructed example using an imaginary token called Calendon: Its current market price is 1 US-Dollar per coin. The Calendon is projected to earn 0.05 US-Dollars per coin and year. Its total value locked in its DeFi protocol is 100 million Dollars. The daily transaction volume is still 10 million Dollars. Finally, the expected earnings growth rate is 20 percent per year.

Using the data given, the following multiples can be determined:

- P/E Ratio = Current Market Price / Projected Earnings per Coin = 1.00 / 0.05 = 20
- P/S Ratio = Current Market Price / Revenue per Coin (assuming the same as earnings P/S Ratio) = 1.00 / 0.05 = 20
- Market Cap-to-Total Value Locked Ratio:

  Market Cap = Current Market Price * Total Circulating Supply (Assuming 100 million coins) Market Cap = 1.00 * 100,000,000 = 100,000,000
  Market Cap-to-TVL Ratio = Market Cap / TVL = 100,000,000 / 100,000,000 = 1

- Network Value-to-Transactions Ratio = Market Cap / Daily Transaction Volume = $100,000,000 / $10,000,000 = 10
- Token Price-to-Earnings Growth Ratio = P/E Ratio / Earnings Growth Rate = 20 / 20% = 1

- Token Velocity (Assuming 1-year holding period) = Annual Transaction Volume / Total Circulating Supply = \$10,000,000 / 100,000,000 = 0.1

5 Digital Assets in a Portfolio

Abstract: Digital asset investments should be incorporated into a comprehensive portfolio strategy encompassing all asset classes. A portfolio represents the collective sum of an investor's assets, irrespective of their specific asset class. Incorporating financial assets, including digital ones, into a portfolio can diversify its holdings or amplify its potential returns, depending on the investor's preferences concerning risk, return, and investment duration. By integrating digital assets within a systematic portfolio approach, investors can better understand their impact across various asset classes. Constructing, sizing, and rebalancing a portfolio should always reflect an investor's objectives and preferences concerning potential returns, risks, and time horizons. Undertaking due diligence is paramount when assembling a well-balanced portfolio.

This section posits that investments in digital assets should be seen in a portfolio approach involving all asset classes. It discusses digital assets as an asset class and explains the steps to allocate investments to specific assets. This section addresses:

- Investment and Portfolio
- Portfolio strategy
- Investment strategy
- Digital assets as venture capital
- Portfolio construction considerations
- Portfolio sizing and rebalancing
- Operational considerations
- First steps in due diligence
- Granular due diligence

5.1 Investment and Portfolio

Investment and portfolio are related concepts referring to gaining access to assets and their fruits. Each of these concepts has a different scope. So far, this Element did not differentiate between them. However, a portfolio approach is superior to singling out specific investments when allocating money to digital assets.

Investment refers to committing money or capital to an asset, security, business venture, or any other endeavor expecting to generate a profit or return on that capital over time. The primary goal of an investment is to grow the initial amount of money or capital put into it.

A portfolio, on the other hand, refers to the collection or combination of multiple investments. It is the combined holdings of various assets an investor or entity owns. For simplification's sake, in this section, the owner and manager of the portfolio are the same agents. Portfolios are created to diversify risk, manage returns, and achieve a particular financial objective.

The purpose of building a portfolio is to spread investments across various asset classes, industries, and regions to reduce the impact of potential losses from any single investment and to capture a certain breadth of value drivers.

Portfolio management balances **risk and return** based on the investor's financial objectives, risk tolerance, and time horizon. These three constitute the portfolio's profile. Sometimes, additional constraints complement the profile. Examples are considerations about taxation, reputation, or values.

Generally, a portfolio holds investments in several **asset classes**. These classes are broad categories of financial instruments or investments with similar characteristics and behave similarly within the financial markets. These classes are used to group different types of assets based on their risk, return potential, correlation with other assets, and overall investment characteristics. Investors often diversify their portfolios by allocating funds across several asset classes to decrease risk and enhance potential returns.

There are asset classes in public markets, such as equities and bonds, and in private markets, for example, private debt and equity, hedge funds, structured products, or real assets. The choice of asset classes and their balance depend on the portfolio's profile and strategy.

Usually, portfolios determine their profile as a starting point. Based on this profile, the portfolio and investment strategies are derived. Part of these strategies is identifying asset classes and methods for accessing them. Next follows portfolio sizing and deploying investments, that is, allocating money to specific investment objects in each asset class. Monitoring and rebalancing complete the portfolio management process. These steps are explained in more detail below, focusing on digital assets.

The portfolio approach for investing in digital assets is more successful than an individual investment because portfolio management allocates money systematically. The market behavior of digital assets is mainly unknown and inconstant. Regarding them at the individual investment level makes them too risky for most investors. On the other hand, risk-prone investors might feel "happy-go-lucky" pricing hipped investments above fair value.

The portfolio approach mitigates these effects by stipulating a profile for the portfolio, considering risk and growth opportunities from the digital asset class and how it influences the whole portfolio. As a systematic approach, it better assesses risk and is more realistic in the valuation of assets than individual investments.

A note on the term **portfolio**: Its use here is in line with the CAIA curriculum referring to the asset-class independent sum of all investments of an agent. The word portfolio can also refer to the sum of an agent's digital assets in different contexts. In both cases, the meaning is the same. It refers to a group of investments. The difference is the aggregation level. It is good practice in investing to take a portfolio view, including all asset classes, to understand the agent's risk-return profile better. This view is taken in this section regarding portfolios (Chambers et al. 2020).

5.2 Portfolio Strategy

The strategy of the consolidated level of a portfolio is a point on the spectrum between diversification and return. Diversification spreads investments across different asset classes, industries, regions, and securities to reduce exposure to any single investment's risk. The core idea behind diversification is that not all investments will perform well simultaneously, and by holding a mix of assets, the overall impact of underperforming investments on the portfolio can be minimized. The return strategy optimizes the portfolio to achieve the highest possible return while considering risk factors. Investors pursuing a return strategy aim to maximize the gains from their investments, seeking higher returns. Digital assets can be an addition to a portfolio. As an asset class or investments, they can add value by furthering diversification or increasing return potential.

Allocating investments to digital assets for **diversifying** a portfolio entails a long-only allocation, which can expand the efficient frontier, enhancing returns for a given level of risk. The efficient frontier of a portfolio is a fundamental concept in modern portfolio theory MPT introduced by Harry Markowitz in the 1950s. It represents the set of optimal portfolios that provide the highest level of expected return for a given level of risk or the lowest level of risk for a given level of expected return. In other words, the efficient frontier maps the trade-off between risk and return for a portfolio.

Digital assets can be used for asset class blending across multiple strategies to diversify. For example, Hedge funds can employ arbitrage, trading, and growth strategies. Venture capitalists invest in coins, tokens, as well as the equity of companies across the digital asset ecosystem. Similarly, distressed investors have expanded their universe to include distressed crypto companies.

Digital assets can also be venture capital complements. Digital asset investments may offer a similarly high-risk, high-return profile complementary to traditional venture capital investments.

A third way to diversify a portfolio with digital assets is employing them as a technology hedge. Given the potential for blockchain and distributed ledger technologies to disintermediate big tech companies, investing in them may offset this obsolescence risk.

Digital assets may also increase the **return potential** of a portfolio. As an emerging asset with substantial uncertainty, they have the potential to provide an asymmetry of returns and risk not available in most other asset classes. As with any new, inefficient, and complicated asset, there are many opportunities for alpha.

As a reminder, the term "inefficient" refers to the market not being knowledgeable about the investment and unable to reflect all information in its pricing. Complicated denotes that specific knowledge about this investment space usually yields higher returns than the market average.

Alpha measures an investment's performance relative to a benchmark index. It indicates the excess return (positive or negative) that an investment generates compared to what would be expected given its level of risk. Popular benchmarks are the Bitwise 10 Crypto Index, the Bloomberg Galaxy Crypto Index, and the One River Size Tilt Index.

5.3 Investment Strategy

In addition to the portfolio-level strategy, there are strategies for access, asset classes, and investments. The former aims at achieving the owner-specific balance of return, risk, and time horizon. The latter describes the way to unlock value by allocating investments. They complement each other, the investment strategy being the operationalization of the portfolio profile.

Level Two of the CAIA's curriculum offers an in-depth discussion of investment strategies fitting portfolio structures. Here is a compilation of the most essential strategies and the place digital assets have in them.

Modern Portfolio Theory: MPT emphasizes diversification to optimize risk and return. It constructs portfolios based on the efficient frontier, seeking to maximize returns for an established level of risk or minimize risk for a specified level of return. The strategy involves allocating assets across different classes and optimizing the asset mix based on historical risk and return data. In such a strategy, digital assets serve as diversifiers and enhancers – see the discussion above.

Core-Satellite Portfolio: This strategy combines a diversified core portfolio of passively managed assets, such as index funds replicators or exchange-traded funds ETFs, with satellite positions in risky assets, such as individual stocks or actively managed funds. The core provides broad market exposure, while the satellites allow for active management and potential alpha generation. Digital assets fit the satellites.

Cash Flow generating Portfolio: This strategy generates income through dividend-paying stocks, bonds, or other income-generating assets. It suits investors seeking a regular income stream. Many DeFi and Web 3.0 applications generate revenue or cash flow.

Growth-Oriented Portfolio: A growth-oriented portfolio emphasizes investments with high growth potential, such as growth stocks or companies in emerging industries. This strategy is more aggressive and suited for investors and portfolios with higher risk tolerance and longer investment horizon. Volatile digital assets or initial coin offerings are typical ways in which digital assets for this strategy. Growth-oriented portfolios can also use leverage and long-short combinations. Consequently, risk management, conceptions of collateralization, and counterparty surveillance are essential.

Value Investing: Value investing involves seeking undervalued assets or companies with strong fundamentals trading at a discount. The goal is to buy assets below their intrinsic value and benefit when the market eventually recognizes their worth. Many digital assets have no intrinsic value. However, some Stablecoins and DeFi have a floor value. If this floor value trades at a considerable discount to the market, value investing is possible.

Index Investing or Passive Investing: This strategy involves constructing a portfolio replicating the performance of a specific market index, for example, the S&P 500. It aims to match market returns rather than outperform them. Index funds and ETFs are popular choices for passive investing. There are some ETFs for digital assets; a portfolio could also construct its own fund with several tokens replicating the popular benchmarks mentioned in the previous section.

Dividend Growth Investing: This strategy invests in companies with a consistent track record of augmenting dividends. The goal is to benefit from both dividend income and potential capital appreciation. Some DeFi and Web 3.0 applications promise both growth in the returns of the DAO and the value of its native token. Alternatively, investors can seek indirect exposure by investing in parent companies developing dapps, games, or payment systems.

Credit Strategies: Lending money to other agents aims to deliver an attractive income stream to the portfolio, accepting the higher risk for achieving it, for example, default risk. The payment of interest rates and loan repayment are the financial incomes in this strategy. A portfolio could lend money to a miner, a DAO, or a parent company developing and maintaining digital assets. The portfolio could also use DeFi to place loans.

Risk Parity: Risk parity allocates assets based on their risk contributions to the overall portfolio rather than their market value. The goal is to balance risk evenly across different asset classes. Digital assets, especially tokens, can be included as risky assets.

5.4 Digital Assets as Venture Capital

Digital Assets are often compared to venture capital. Venture capital strategies aim to deliver an attractive growth profile to a portfolio and take considerable risk to do so. These assets might be more appropriate for agents seeking growth and willing to take on substantial risk. The assets in these strategies seek capital appreciation and generally have the highest risk relative to most other strategies. A critical characteristic of venture capital is the lifecycle of investments.

Early in the lifecycle, an investment, usually a company, is unprofitable and requires significant fixed investment from the venture capitalist. However, as the company builds scale, the profitability increases. The path to viability and profitability is known as the J-curve.

In the **early stages of the J-curve**, investments "burn" capital and do not yield any returns. In order words, the net returns are negative in the first three to five years of venture investments. Successful enterprises make it through these periods to finally become profitable in the later stages of the curve and distribute profits to shareholders, but not all investments survive. For this reason, the early stage of the curve is informally called the "Valley of Death."

Most of the digital asset ecosystem resides in the Valley of Death, at the bottom of the J-curve. The J-curve is especially relevant for digital assets even in favorable market conditions. For example, in 2021, more than 3,000 listed tokens failed despite a broader rise in digital asset prices (CAIA 2023).

Even if venture capital and digital assets are different, the comparison is helpful to highlight two aspects. First, investing in digital assets involves understanding their value proposition, their governance, and their technology, in short, their business case. Second, such an investment comes with a timewise lock-in. These aspects show that many investments in digital assets are not liquid and involve knowledge, both solid indicators for potential alpha.

While the comparison may be helpful, there are essential differences between the traditional venture capital model and digital assets markets. The most significant difference is that venture capital is centralized in funding, whereas many digital assets seek to be decentralized.

Where digital assets deviate from traditional markets is in their decentralized nature. In rare instances, protocols can be launched with no outside capital, as for Bitcoin. More generally, a certain portion of tokens is made available to investors with a long phase of capital locked. Usually, this phase lasts around seven years. The tokens may actively trade, but venture investors provide

longer-term capital to support project development while investing at a discounted price. Over time, ownership becomes more dispersed, and decision-making becomes more decentralized through DAOs and other mechanisms.

Presently, venture capital is the most common and, typically, the first approach for institutional investors. Venture capitalists view crypto as an investment in future technology with large addressable markets and wish to invest in the growth of this ecosystem. The digital asset ecosystem is broad, and within venture capital, there is specialization, including payments, smart contract platforms, DeFi, Centralized Finance (CeFi), Gaming, Metaverse, social media, NFTs, Stablecoins, and Infrastructure.

5.5 Portfolio Construction Considerations

There are several elements to consider when constructing a portfolio. Next to the strategic dimensions mentioned above, there are specifics of digital assets:

- Ownership
- Access vehicles
- Asset cycles
- Portfolio sizing and rebalancing (see next section)

As in Section 4, these specifics apply, in principle, differently to each use case of digital assets. However, most discussion focuses on tokens as primary use cases or necessary basis for the functioning of a decentralized application. This section discusses the specifics mentioned above with an eye on tokens cautioning this narrow view.

An investor can own digital assets in three ways: **direct token**, **third-party**, and **stock ownership**.

Direct token ownership is the most straightforward approach to investing in digital assets. Ownership can occur by executing transactions or by validating them. Executing a transaction requires directly buying or selling the digital assets' tokens. Alternatively, transaction validators, such as Bitcoin mining and Ethereum staking, can be a way for agents to earn and own tokens. Token ownership is akin to owning and retaining custody of a stock certificate.

Third-party ownership is ownership through a service provider, such as a custodian, exchange, or brokerage firm. Using a service provider still allows for direct exposure to digital assets but provides additional protections through rules, regulations, and regular audits. Third-party ownership is typically how most portfolios own their assets. They may be investors, but the assets are typically held or custodied through a third party. Legally, it is not ownership but custody.

The third approach is owning **shares of public or private companies** that engage with digital assets. It is the most indirect approach but may work for agents seeking to enter the space in a familiar format.

Access vehicles usually apply when agents don't invest directly and on a case-by-case basis. From a portfolio perspective, the suitability of the vehicle depends on the volume of investment, the agent's preference regarding in- or outsourcing, and the agent's overall preferences for exposure. Traditional access vehicles also used in the digital assets' space are investment trusts, exchange-traded products, comingled investment vehicles, and separately managed accounts.

Investment trusts and exchange-traded products are both traded electronically, like individual securities. However, the major difference is that investment trusts are closed-end funds, and exchange-traded products are open-end funds. Commingled investment vehicles pool capital from multiple investors, like hedge funds or venture capital funds. These vehicles are already familiar to agents who invest in alternative investments. These funds allow broad exposure but may have higher fees than other vehicles.

Separately managed accounts SMAs provide a way of owning digital assets or strategies managed by a professional without having other parties' capital alongside. The benefit of SMAs is their direct ownership of the underlying securities and the ability to customize the portfolio. However, some SMAs require higher minimum investments than other fund vehicles and more operational set-up than other vehicles like investment trusts or exchange-traded products.

Another specific of digital assets is their **cycles**. They are usually referred to as seasons. The CAIA differentiates four seasons in the cycle: A crypto fall occurs during a large and lasting decline of 30 percent or more in asset prices. A crypto winter starts after a fall and ends after a 50 percent retracement to the past high. A crypto spring is the initial stage of a price recovery. In the crypto summer, the markets and prices reach new highs at the risk of overheating.

Different strategies deal differently with each season: Income Strategies provide income streams with lower volatility but without much investment upside. It can act as a safe harbor during falls and winters but is also highly dependent on collateral and counterparties. Credit is the hardest hit during the fall but can perform well during the spring. Venture capital tends to do well during spring but suffers greatly in the fall and winter. However, more tactical active strategies may protect on the downside but also have limited upside.

It is important to tie a **portfolio's allocation** to the goals and objectives of the agent and how the underlying investments are used to achieve them. These goals may include a combination of growth, income, capital preservation, and inflation protection. As reviewed above, many digital asset strategies align with different combinations of these objectives.

5.6 Portfolio Sizing and Rebalancing

Portfolio sizing and rebalancing are essential considerations for agents entering digital asset investments. Portfolio sizing refers to determining how much of the total investment capital to allocate to different digital assets within a portfolio. It involves deciding the proportion or percentage of each asset's portfolio.

When **sizing** a portfolio, allocators must consider risk tolerance, asset correlation, market outlook, and investment horizon. This process aims to determine the target allocation per the portfolio's profile.

Usually, the investment horizon is determined on the portfolio level. However, a specific its specific determination for digital assets can be beneficial, primarily when a portfolio invests in such assets with different timeframes. Risk tolerance is also generally defined on a portfolio level. However, digital assets have higher volatility than most other classes. A higher allocation might result in more significant fluctuations in the portfolio's value.

On the other hand, most digital assets have a lower correlation with other asset classes. Diversifying across assets with low or negative correlations can reduce overall portfolio risk. Additionally, the market outlook for many digital assets is positive. This outlook can be done by using valuation methods in a mosaic approach – see Section 4 – and consulting external research for fundamental analysis, market trends, and technological developments.

Research has shown that an appropriate allocation to digital assets should be at most 5 percent of the portfolios before the risk profile becomes dominated by it. Limiting the portfolio size also protects the portfolio from large risk events. Digital asset portfolio construction is important, but sizing can be a powerful risk mitigator (CAIA 2023).

Research has also shown that portfolios starting with a limited scope of digital assets, Bitcoin and Ether, or the ten tokens with the largest capitalization, best manage portfolio construction and sizing.

Rebalancing involves periodically adjusting the allocations of different assets within the portfolio to bring them back to their intended proportions. Over time, the market performance of various assets can vary, causing the initial allocation to deviate. Rebalancing helps maintain the desired risk profile and ensures the portfolio aligns with the investment objectives.

Usually, the rebalancing process involves periodically reviewing the portfolio's performance and allocation comparing them to the target allocation. Suppose the current allocation significantly, that is, outside a predetermined bandwidth (e.g., 5 percent deviation from the target allocation), deviates from the target allocation. In that case, the holdings are adjusted by buying or selling assets accordingly.

The frequency of rebalancing can vary depending on the portfolio's strategy. Some investors rebalance monthly, quarterly, annually, or when a specific threshold is breached. The more frequent rebalancing occurs, the higher the costs of portfolio management. The less frequently it takes place, the more tactical the allocation becomes and the more it might deviate from the strategy.

The benefits of rebalancing in the context of digital assets include controlling risk exposure, taking advantage of market inefficiencies, and reducing the impact of emotional decision-making during volatile market conditions.

5.7 Operational Considerations

Next to questions directly relating to the economics of investing, there are more operational questions most portfolios also need to address:

- Regulation
- Custody
- Taxation

Segments of the digital asset space are already **regulated**. For example, centralized exchanges are regulated by the Bank Secrecy Act in the United States. Additionally, exchange service providers must register with the Financial Crimes Enforcement Network FinCEN, implement anti-money laundering processes, maintain appropriate records, and submit reports to the authorities. In many instances, securities laws apply to digital wallets and exchanges. On the other hand, the digital asset space is still mostly unregulated.

Since its inception, there has been a strong streak against regulating digital assets. The principle of decentralization espoused and implemented by most agents in the space includes self-governance and the rejection of regulation issued by centralized stances. However, portfolio and their holders continue to be regulated even if digital assets deliver on their value-adding promise of doing away with regulation. In any case, knowing whether regulations impose constraints on how portfolios allocate their investments is important.

Digital assets have no physical manifestation – they exist as digital entries in a virtual, shared ledger. The recent emergence of these assets has prompted a reexamination of the concepts of ownership and **custody**.

Since the 1970s, the move from paper-based securities to electronic registries maintained by central securities depositories has led to substituting direct by indirect holding of assets. The meaning of ownership differs across jurisdictions and even more for digital objects.

Third-party custodians mostly hold traditional assets, and, in the United States, financial advisers must use "qualified custodians" to safeguard client assets. These third parties offer security, standardization rules, and insurance.

There are unique considerations for the digital asset ecosystem. Funds are held in digital wallets, which come from various levels of security. Cryptographic keys that identify ownership need to be appropriately secured. Various protections have emerged with the maturing of the industry. An example is the requirement of multiple digital signatures to initiate a transfer.

Digital assets are **taxable**. But tax frameworks are incomplete. A simple rule of thumb is comparing digital assets with the traditional equivalent. If an agent generates yield from lending in DeFi, it is akin to income. There is a conservative rule of thumb to consider whether a digital asset is taxable. If the asset resembles a traditional asset, it is safe to assume that it will be treated the same way the traditional asset is for purposes of regulation and taxation.

5.8 First Steps in Due Diligence

Due diligence is a comprehensive, systematic, documented investigation to assess an investment's viability, risks, and potential benefits. Due diligence aims to muster all relevant information about the subject under consideration, allowing the agent to make well-informed decisions based on facts.

Especially for investors and portfolio allocators entering the digital assets space, the following first steps initiate due diligence:

- Spending time with traditional asset managers who have developed digital asset knowledge. They are more likely to speak the language of traditional investment management and this new technology, which may help translate between the two worlds.
- Reading whitepapers. Each digital asset has a whitepaper explaining how it works, its use case, and how it creates value. Comparing these whitepapers adds to knowledge and experience, helping to develop a benchmark.
- Start by learning the use case, risk profile, fair price valuation, and general behavior patterns with small amounts of capital. It includes engaging with wallets, conducting DeFi transactions, or making payments.
- Spending time in the channels where dialogue and discussions about digital assets happen. In many ways, cryptocurrencies and digital assets exist in areas not traditional to most finance processes. These channels include

specialized purveyors of research, Twitter, podcasts, crypto-specific press, blogs, discord channels, and Telegram.

- Deploying through intermediaries like a fund of funds or using a consultant. They may diversify across geography, size, and sectors.

As in any inefficient and complicated space, according to the efficient market theory, there are charlatans in the digital asset space. They try to misuse the inability of the market to gather information and reveal them in prices not to generate alpha but to their own advantage at the expense of the portfolios. Caution, common sense, and validation of data and counterparties or partners are necessary.

While learning the language of digital assets may seem intimidating, during the advent of investing in Hedge Funds, Leveraged Buyouts, and Venture Capital, different skills were (and still are) required compared to traditional investment management. Just as when those strategies were emerging, in the case of digital assets, investors must be prepared for new challenges and unfamiliar territory. Rather than thinking of digital assets as uncertain and risky, it may be helpful to consider that something similar is happening with digital assets, as with other new asset classes that were no less uncertain and less risky. Learning new technology and research methods will still benefit even if digital asset investments are not made.

5.9 Granular Due Diligence

CAIA favors this more granular approach to digital assets. After investors or portfolio aggregators familiarize themselves with digital assets through the first steps of due diligence, they can take this more granular approach by engaging with a specialized manager. Important questions to focus on when researching dedicated managers include:

- What are the economic incentives of managers?
- In which use cases and distributed ledgers are they involved?
- How do the various participants in these use cases and blockchains fit together?
- To what extent has a dedicated manager's team worked through multiple digital assets market cycles?
- Are there people on the dedicated manager's team with risk and portfolio management backgrounds?

According to CAIA (CAIA 2023), additional factors to discuss with investment managers when investing in the digital asset space are:

- Use of Service Providers

- Is the dedicated manager utilizing well-known legal, fund administration, and auditors?
- Independently confirm the service relationships and ask questions regarding the arrangement and terms of service.
- Ensure monthly transparency reports can be made available

- Operational Risks

  - Understand how decisions are authorized and executed
  - Look for dedicated functions to ensure the separation of duties
  - Do they use qualified custodians?
  - Understand the use and management of private keys and multi-signature wallets.
  - Does the manager employ asset sweeping?
  - How can investors verify assets?
  - How does the fund audit assets?
  - Are there automated liquidation risks investors should be aware of?
  - How well-defined are the compliance procedures?

- Investment Strategy Risks

  - What assets are being used?
  - Is the strategy more susceptible to black swan / exogenous events?
  - What is the level of latency, and how does that impact execution and liquidity?
  - What is the role of leverage?
  - Is the strategy deployed on Decentralized Exchanges (DEX), Centralized Exchanges (CEX), or both, and how do the risks differ across exchange types?
  - Transparency – Are wallet addresses public to view transaction history?
  - What is the valuation process, and how are the assets valued
  - How are investment opportunities sourced? Have they built a network to gain early access and proprietary deal flow?
  - What elements contributed to their ability to close previous investments? Why do founders want to partner with this fund manager?
  - Does the fund size match the strategy and opportunity set?

- Reputational Risk

  - Review social media for historical accuracy and firm evolution
  - Review social media for lifestyle creep. How is the team spending their time?
  - Review conflict of interest disclosures.
  - Reference checks and background checks are strongly encouraged to help mitigate reputation risk.

- Regulatory Risk

  - With considerable regulatory uncertainty, what type of scenario planning has the team done? Do they have a road map regarding the evolution of regulations?

- Failure Risks

  - How does the manager evaluate counterparty risk?
  - How does the manager mitigate hacking risk?

Examining how to invest in digital assets, from holding liquid tokens directly to locking up capital for many years in illiquid venture structures, is important. Recognizing that illiquid investments can quickly turn liquid via a token sale, it is important to ask an investment manager what type of investment vehicle is being used and why it is being used. Additionally, investors should ask about the full range of vehicles on offer, as it is common to have several. Specific points to check are:
Liquid Market Investments

- Coins/Tokens

  - To date, most institutional investors have avoided direct coin/token investing due to the challenges of self-custody
  - Qualified Custodians help reduce the complexity of direct ownership and may be a preferred option for institutions interested in holding coins/tokens.

- Long-only Funds

  - Various fund options exist, from passive to active, public and private vehicles. Important factors to evaluate are fees, custody, and liquidity.
  - The availability of spot cryptocurrency ETFs varies by country. Thus far, five countries (Switzerland, Germany, Canada, UAE, and Australia) have approved spot bitcoin ETF applications, while the United States continues to deny applications (although it did approve ETFs holding cryptocurrency futures contracts)

- Hedge Funds

  - The two most common strategies are Market Neutral and Multistrategy

- Public Equities

  - While the availability of crypto-related public stocks varies by region, there are a growing number of businesses focused on digital assets that are publicly traded.

- It is important to understand what idiosyncratic risks are associated with each and the level of correlation the business has with the digital asset ecosystem and specific cryptocurrencies.

Illiquid (primarily venture capital)

- As previously noted, investment due diligence should encompass both the traditional venture-related due diligence questions as well as the crypto-oriented questions.
- Funds may invest in tokens only, or the manager may invest in tokens along with an equity stake in the underlying business.
- While the fund may be illiquid, the holdings may vary in liquidity. How does the fund manage liquidity? When an investment becomes liquid, do they sell it, hold it, or some combination?

6 Conclusion: A Framework for Investing in Digital Assets

6.1 Investment Goals & Objectives

- *Risk Appetite*: Determine the risk tolerance of the investor. Digital assets can be highly volatile, and not all investors have the stomach for such risk.
- *Return Expectations*: Understand the potential returns the investor seeks. Some digital assets have the potential for high returns but come with more significant risks.
- *Investment Horizon*: Consider the period for which the investor plans to hold the digital asset. Some assets might be more suited for short-term trading, while others might be more suitable for long-term holding.

6.2 Due Diligence on the Digital Asset

- *Asset Background:* Understand the history, the team behind the digital asset, its use case, and its adoption trajectory. Refer to the whitepaper.
- *Technology Assessment:* Examine the underlying technology. Is it blockchain, another type of DLT, or something else? What about the security features?
- *Regulatory Stance:* Review the current regulatory environment for the asset in the investor's jurisdiction and, if applicable, globally.

6.3 Market Analysis

- *Liquidity*: Ensure the asset is traded in a volume that allows easy entry and exit.
- *Volatility*: Analyze the asset's price fluctuations. Some investors might want to avoid excessively volatile assets.
- *Market Sentiment*: Gauge the prevailing sentiment towards the asset. Are experts
- bullish or bearish on the use case (not the value)?

6.4 Portfolio Fit

- *Diversification:* Check how the digital asset correlates with other assets in the portfolio. Ideally, it should provide diversification benefits.
- *Allocation Size:* Decide on the percentage of the portfolio to allocate to the digital asset. Even bullish investors might choose to limit exposure due to the inherent risks.

6.5 Risk Management

- *Stop-Loss & Take-Profit Points:* Establish levels at which investors sell to cut losses or take profits.
- *Review & Rebalance:* Periodically review the performance of the digital asset. If it has grown to dominate the portfolio, consider rebalancing.

6.6 Exclusion Criteria

- *Unfavorable Due Diligence*: Any red flags during the asset background check or technology assessment might be grounds for exclusion.
- *Regulatory Concerns*: If an asset faces significant regulatory hurdles, it might be best to exclude it.
- *High Correlation*: If the digital asset correlates too closely with another asset in the portfolio without providing better returns or other benefits, consider excluding it.

6.7 Continuous Monitoring & Review

- *Performance Tracking*: Continuously monitor the performance of the digital asset relative to expectations.

- *News & Updates*: Stay updated with any news related to the digital asset or the broader market. Significant developments could be a cue to revise the asset's position in the portfolio.
- *Feedback Loop*: Regularly reflect on decisions made (both inclusions and exclusions) to refine the framework and the decision-making process.

Bibliography

Agarwal, Nipun. "How to obtain the fair value for cryptocurrency and digital assets." *International Journal of Blockchains and Cryptocurrencies* 3.1 (2022): 16–23.

CAIA. *Digital Assets Microcredential*. 2023. https://caia.org/unifi-digital-assets-microcredential.

Chambers, Donald R., Hossein B. Kazemi, Keith H. Black, and CAIA Association. *Alternative Investments: An Allocator's Approach*. Hoboken: John Wiley & Sons, 2020.

Dhillon, Robinpreet, and Ehsan Nikbakht. "Cryptoassets in a portfolio context." In H. Kent Baker, Hugo Benedetti, Ehsan Nikbakht, Sean Stein Smith (eds.), *The Emerald Handbook on Cryptoassets: Investment Opportunities and Challenges*. Bingley: Emerald, 2023. 185–198.

Drake, Pamela Peterson, and Frank J. Fabozzi. *The Basics of Finance: An Introduction to Financial Markets, Business Finance, and Portfolio Management*. Hoboken: John Wiley & Sons, 2010.

El Ioini, Nabil, and Claus Pahl. "A review of distributed ledger technologies." *On the Move to Meaningful Internet Systems. OTM 2018 Conferences, Proceedings, Part II*. Springer, 2018: 277–288.

Fama, Eugene. *The Fama Portfolio: Selected Papers of Eugene F. Fama*. Chicago: University of Chicago Press, 2017.

Gerunov, Anton. "Risk in digital assets." *Risk Analysis for the Digital Age* (2022): 81–114.

Glas, Tobias. "How to incorporate characteristics into the portfolio construction process." In Tobias Glas (ed.), *Asset Pricing and Investment Styles in Digital Assets: A Comparison with Traditional Asset Classes*. Cham: Springer International, 2022. 175–186.

Goutte, Stéphane, Khaled Guesmi, and Samir Saadi, eds. *Cryptofinance: A New Currency for a New Economy*. Singapore: World Scientific, 2021.

Hamilton, Marc. "Blockchain distributed ledger technology: An introduction and focus on smart contracts." *Journal of Corporate Accounting & Finance* 31.2 (2020): 7–12.

Hougan, Matt, and David Lawant. *Cryptoassets: The guide to bitcoin, blockchain, and cryptocurrency for investment professionals*. Charlottesville: CFA Institute Research Foundation, .

Kaal, Wulf A., Samuel R. Evans, and Hayley A. Howe. "Digital asset valuation." *Richmond Journal of Law and Technology* 28 (2021): 657–699.

Kim, Sun-Woong. "Portfolio diversification effect of digital assets." *Journal of Digital Contents Society* 22.6 (2021): 1015–1023.

Labazova, Olga, Erol Kazan, Tobias Dehling "Managing Blockchain Systems and Applications: A Process Model for Blockchain Configurations." *arXiv preprint arXiv:2105.02118* (2021).

Maull, Roger, Phil Godsiff, Catherine Mulligan. "Distributed ledger technology: Applications and implications." *Strategic Change* 26.5 (2017): 481–489.

Ozili, Peterson K. "Decentralized finance research and developments around the world." *Journal of Banking and Financial Technology* 6.2 (2022): 117–133.

Ragnedda, Massimo, and Giuseppe Destefanis. *Blockchain and Web 3.0.* London: Routledge, 2019.

Rikken, Olivier, Marijn Janssen, and Zenlin Kwee. "Governance challenges of blockchain and decentralized autonomous organizations." *Information Polity* 24.4 (2019): 397–417.

Ruan, Keyun. *Digital Asset Valuation and Cyber Risk Measurement: Principles of Cybernomics.* Cambridge MA: Academic Press, 2019.

Rudman, Riaan. "Web 3.0: Governance, risks, and safeguards." *Journal of Applied Business Research (JABR)* 31.3 (2015): 1037–1056.

Schneider, Henrique. "Cryptocurrencies: The sages and the charlatans." *Geopolitical Information Services* (2023). www.gisreportsonline.com/r/cryptocurrencies-the-sages-and-the-charlatans/.

Sehra, Avtar, Richard Cohen, and Vic Arulchandran. "On cryptocurrencies, digital assets, and private money." *Journal of Payments Strategy & Systems* 12.1 (2018): 13–32.

Zetzsche, Dirk A., Douglas W. Arner, and Ross P. Buckley. "Decentralized finance (defi)." *Journal of Financial Regulation* 6 (2020): 172–203.

Zīle, Kaspars, and Renāte Strazdiņa. "Blockchain use cases and their feasibility." *Applied Computer Systems* 23.1 (2018): 12–20.

Acknowledgments

An important note of thanks: This Element would not have been possible without the support of this series editor, JC Spender. Discussions with officers from CAIA and many students writing a thesis about digital assets greatly benefitted this work. Jörg Richard and Valon Hasanaj's reviews were precious for improving this argument. Valon is the "true" author of the concluding section.

Cambridge Elements ⹀

Business Strategy

J.-C. Spender
Kozminski University

J.-C. Spender is a research Professor, Kozminski University. He has been active in the business strategy field since 1971 and is the author or co-author of 7 books and numerous papers. His principal academic interest is in knowledge-based theories of the private sector firm, and managing them.

Advisory Board

About the Series

Business strategy's reach is vast, and important too since wherever there is business activity there is strategizing. As a field, strategy has a long history from medieval and colonial times to today's developed and developing economies. This series offers a place for interesting and illuminating research including industry and corporate studies, strategizing in service industries, the arts, the public sector, and the new forms of Internet-based commerce. It also covers today's expanding gamut of analytic techniques.

Cambridge Elements ☰

Business Strategy

Printed in the United States
by Baker & Taylor Publisher Services